Martin C. Brown
Don Jones, series editor

D1622147

Microsoft
IIS 6

DELTA GUIDE

SAMS   800 East 96th St., Indianapolis, Indiana, 46240 USA

Microsoft IIS 6 Delta Guide

International Standard Book Number: 0-672-32575-6

Library of Congress Catalog Card Number: 2003110396

Printed in the United States of America

First Printing: November 2003

06   05   04   03   4   3   2   1

Trademarks

All terms mentioned in this book that are known to be trademarks or service marks have been appropriately capitalized. Sams Publishing cannot attest to the accuracy of this information. Use of a term in this book should not be regarded as affecting the validity of any trademark or service mark.

Warning and Disclaimer

Every effort has been made to make this book as complete and as accurate as possible, but no warranty or fitness is implied. The information provided is on an "as is" basis. The author and the publisher shall have neither liability nor responsibility to any person or entity with respect to any loss or damages arising from the information contained in this book.

Bulk Sales

Sams Publishing offers excellent discounts on this book when ordered in quantity for bulk purchases or special sales. For more information, please contact

U.S. Corporate and Government Sales

1-800-382-3419

corpsales@pearsontechgroup.com

For sales outside of the U.S., please contact

International Sales

1-317-428-3341

international@pearsontechgroup.com

Executive Editor
Candace Hall

Acquisitions Editor
Loretta Yates

Development Editor
Songlin Qiu

Managing Editor
Charlotte Clapp

Project Editor
Sheila Schroeder

Series Editor
Don Jones

Copy Editor
Rhonda Tinch-Mize

Indexer
Ken Johnson

Proofreader
Tracy Donhardt

Technical Editor
Bill Hubbard

Team Coordinator
Cindy Teeters

Multimedia Developer
Dan Scherf

Interior Designer
Gary Adair

Cover Designer
Gary Adair

Contents at a Glance

Table of Contents

Foreword

IIS was almost a stealth success for Microsoft. Version 3.0 in particular, with its introduction of Active Server Pages (ASP), probably did more to put Microsoft on the Internet than any other product the company had produced at the time. The ease with which IIS could be deployed, and the ease with which developers could create ASP applications, quickly made IIS 3.0 the top commercial Web server product on the market. Literally, tens of thousands of Web servers ran IIS, and Microsoft rode that wave of success and introduced a number of successful products that built on IIS, including Exchange's Outlook Web Access, Site Server and Commerce Server, the Microsoft Commercial Internet System, and many more.

IIS 4.0 was introduced for Windows NT Server 4.0, and IIS 5.0 was included with Windows 2000. Windows XP included a minor upgrade, IIS 5.1, and now we're looking at IIS 6.0, bundled with Windows Server 2003. A *lot* has changed since IIS first became a success. In fact, many of the changes in IIS 6.0 are a direct reaction to IIS' overall success as a product; IIS 6.0's new architecture, for example, is designed to cope with even greater numbers of Web site users and to provide better security and application stability.

In *Windows Server 2003 Delta Guide,* my coauthor and I introduced IIS 6.0 and tried to cover its new features as best we could in a single chapter. We quickly realized that we were in over our heads, and that an entire book on IIS 6.0 was needed. With his extensive background in Web server technology, Martin C. Brown was an ideal choice to write that book, and you hold the results in your hand. This book is everything the *Delta Guide* series was meant to be, and will provide experienced Windows and IIS administrators with the fastest possible means of understanding and utilizing the many new and changed features in IIS 6.0.

It's fitting that the second *Delta Guide* should cover IIS because the *Delta Guide* series has been a sort of "stealth success" in its own right. I'm delighted with the reader response to *Windows Server 2003 Delta Guide,* which clearly demonstrates that readers are tired of paying for the same old text over and over again just to learn what's new and changed in Microsoft products. To help satisfy your thirst for more details on what's new and changed, I've created a Web site and discussion forum at www.deltaguideseries.com. There, you will find book updates, additional details on new and changed technologies, and much more. Contributors include *Delta Guide* authors and other industry luminaries, and you're sure to find something useful there.

Now, sit back and turn the page. You've found the fastest, most reliable way to quickly upgrade your IIS administration skills to cover IIS 6.0.

Don Jones
Series editor and founding partner of BrainCore.Net

About the Author

Martin C. Brown is a former IT director with experience in cross-platform integration. A keen developer, he has produced dynamic sites for blue-chip customers, including HP and Oracle, and is the technical director of Foodware.net. Now a freelance writer and consultant, MC, as he is better known, works closely with Microsoft as a Subject Matter Expert (SME), is the LAMP technologies editor for *LinuxWorld* magazine, has regular article spots on ServerWatch.com and IBM DeveloperWorks, is a core member of the AnswerSquad.com team, and has written books such as *XML Processing with Perl, Python, and PHP* and portions of *Apache 2.0: The Complete Reference*. MC can be contacted at questions@mcslp.com, or through his Web site at www.mcslp.com.

Dedication

To Sharon, my advisor, best friend, and wife.

Acknowledgments

When you sit in your study, on your bed, in your lounge, or—if you are lucky enough—out in your garden writing your book, you sometimes begin to feel like you are the only person devoted to completing the book. I've found this especially so very late at night!

In truth, of course, a great many people are involved behind the scenes who take what I write and turn it into the dead-tree book you have in your hands. Before I even start writing, it's down to my agent, Neil Salkind, to handle all the negotiations. Neil continues to do a stunning job in this respect, and I wouldn't have done this book, or many others, without his help. I also need to thank Don Jones, the series editor, for believing in me and the review team for giving me the enthusiasm to continue.

Candace Hall at Sams needs to be thanked for agreeing to take on the project and who understood when I had to fly 12,000 miles to Seattle for Microsoft. Twice. In the middle of the project.

Loretta Yates at Sams needs extra special thanks for helping to keep me on track and complete the project, as well as for stepping in mid-project as Candace left for more important matters.

Thanks to the project team at Sams who take the final manuscript and go through the different stages of development, copy, and production, including Songlin Qiu, Rhonda Tinch-Mize, Sheila Schroeder, and anybody else I've never met, but who does a stunning job all the same!

Finally, I need to thank those wonderful guys at Microsoft's certification division for providing some much needed help and input when I needed it. To the guys at GrandMasters, like Ron Thomas and Richard Kobylka, who provided much fun in the middle of the project while I was in Seattle, and to the SME teams who helped keep the process fun, thanks.

We Want to Hear from You!

As the reader of this book, *you* are our most important critic and commentator. We value your opinion and want to know what we're doing right, what we could do better, what areas you'd like to see us publish in, and any other words of wisdom you're willing to pass our way.

As an executive editor for Sams Publishing, I welcome your comments. You can email or write me directly to let me know what you did or didn't like about this book—as well as what we can do to make our books better.

Please note that I cannot help you with technical problems related to the topic of this book. We do have a User Services group, however, where I will forward specific technical questions related to the book.

When you write, please be sure to include this book's title and author as well as your name, email address, and phone number. I will carefully review your comments and share them with the author and editors who worked on the book.

Email: feedback@samspublishing.com

Mail: Candace Hall
         Executive Editor
         Sams Publishing
         800 East 96th Street
         Indianapolis, IN 46240 USA

For more information about this book or another Sams Publishing title, visit our Web site at www.samspublishing.com. Type the ISBN (excluding hyphens) or the title of a book in the Search field to find the page you're looking for.

Introduction

Who Should Read This Book

The whole purpose of this book is to get you up to speed as quickly as possible on the new features in IIS 6.0—the version of the Internet Information Server that comes with Windows Server 2003. Although, theoretically, you could use this to help you learn IIS 6, a lot of items and features simply are not covered because they haven't changed since the earlier versions. In short, if you don't already know IIS 4 or IIS 5, you need to start elsewhere.

However, this doesn't mean that you need to be an expert. I've provided a combination of background information, pointers, and a number of online articles to help you understand the new system as much as possible.

How to Use This Book

The book is divided into chapters that look at specific areas of IIS 6, including securing, performance, management, and migration techniques. There is no real sequence to the book, but you will almost certainly find it easier to read the earlier chapters first because the most significant IIS 6 changes are covered there. You will also find a great deal of additional information on the Delta Guide series Web site at www.deltaguideseries.com. The Web site also contains late-breaking information, a discussion forum about this book, and information on other books in the series.

After that, use the table of contents to look up the specific chapter that covers what you need to know.

As you're reading, you will notice a number of special elements:

NOTE ENTRIES
Notes are designed to give you little pieces of information to help you understand an item, highlight a particularly important point, or point you toward some additional source of information.

CAUTION ITEM

Occasionally, there is an item or feature that could cause problems if used incorrectly or without care. I'll use these caution items to help prevent a potential disaster, or highlight where a particular solution or system doesn't work either in the way you expect or in the way you have become accustomed to in previous editions.

TIP ITEM

Tips are those handy hints for how you can make better use of the system. These have usually been learned from personal experience and should help you manage the system and save time in the long run.

 ## DON'S TIPS

This is where series creator Don Jones gets to mention a quick tip. These will usually be tidbits from Don's consulting experience that might help you avoid a snag or make something more efficient.

 ## WEB RESOURCE

For more background information about a particular item, either to remind you how the existing system works, or for more in-depth detail on particular areas, all the chapters have additional online articles. The articles are referred to by a unique article ID. You can find them by going to the Delta Guide series Web site at www.deltaguideseries.com and enter article ID **A020701**, for example.

▶ When I want to point you in the direction of another chapter that contains more relevant details, you will see a cross reference like this one: **see** Chapter 2, "Architecture and Execution," **p. xxx**.

Introducing IIS 6

1

Internet Information Server 6.0 (IIS 6) is the latest incarnation of the Internet services component of Windows Server 2003. Windows Server 2003 is the most recent release of Microsoft's line of server operating systems based on the Windows NT (New Technology) code base. Windows Server 2003 builds on the success of both Windows NT and Windows 2000, while also incorporating certain features and enhancements made available in the desktop operating system Windows XP. Both Windows Server 2003 and XP share the same code base; both are derivatives of the system originally code named Whistler.

 WEB RESOURCE

For more information on the history of IIS, visit www.samspublishing.com and enter this book's ISBN number (no hyphens or parenthesis) in the Search field; then click the book cover image to access the book details page. Click the Web Resources link in the More Information section and locate article ID# **020101**.

IT'S JUST "IIS"

For the sake of brevity, I refer to Internet Information Server as IIS throughout the rest of the book. When referring to IIS in general, I just use IIS, but when referring to a specific version, I use the corresponding version number as well; that is, IIS 4, IIS 5, or IIS 6.

In many ways, IIS 6 is a complete redevelopment of the IIS platform, but without losing much of the flexibility, power, or feature set of the core IIS product. Much of what you know about IIS—how to manage it, build Web sites, and provide IIS-based services—remains the same.

However, many areas have been updated and expanded, and this has inevitably brought about changes to certain aspects of the administration of your IIS installation.

 DOES IT ALL LOOK THE SAME?

Don't be fooled by how similar IIS' administrative interface looks to prior versions—IIS 6 really is brand new under the hood, and the differences make it both more stable and more secure.

Supported Features

IIS is, in fact, a generic term that covers a number of different servers and services—all of which are responsible for one or more of the following: transferring files, supporting user communication, or publishing information.

IIS is composed of five main components handled by a number of service hosts and individually supported through a number of primary DLL components. You can see the full list in Table 1.1.

TABLE 1.1   Components and Executables for IIS

Service	Primary DLL Component	Service Host
World Wide Publishing service (WWW service)	Iisw3adm.dll	Svchost.exe
File Transfer Protocol service (FTP service)	Ftpsvc2.dll	Inetinfo.exe
Simple Mail Transfer Protocol service (SMTP service)	Smtpsvc.dll	Inetinfo.exe
Network News Transfer Protocol service (NNTP service)	Nntpsvc.dll	Inetinfo.exe
IIS Admin service	Iisadmin.dll	Inetinfo.exe

Most people will consider the WWW service the primary component of the IIS system, and it will be a core consideration in this book.

For the remainder of this book, I show you the new and changed features in IIS 6. However, there are four main threads to the various improvements made in this latest revision of IIS:

Performance—A brand new method of execution for the IIS component improves performance for static pages, dynamic pages, and especially in the realm of multiple-site installations hosted from a single machine.

Stability—The new execution model also protects individual processes so that problems with a client or a third-party application do not slow down or crash the entire system. An improved Quality of Service (QoS) system can be tuned to improve the reliability of the system without having to manually adjust and optimize different components.

Security—Both the underlying Windows Server 2003 system and the IIS component have had their security systems updated. New locking modes for the IIS component improve basic security, and clients can be authenticated through new ASP.NET, Passport, and delegated authentication models.

Management—The IIS MMC snap-in has been updated not only to handle the new features, but also to make it easier to manage sites—particularly when using multiple virtual sites or when hosting a number of domains. The IIS metabase is now stored entirely in XML, making it easy to modify, update, and replicate configurations.

Taking a wider view of the Application Server role that Microsoft has now applied to the servers that support IIS, we also need to include the integration with .NET technologies. Windows Server 2003 comes with the .NET Framework pre-installed, making it the ideal platform for providing Web services and applications using .NET technology.

 .NET FRAMEWORK VERSIONS

Windows Server 2003 comes with version 1.1 of the .NET Framework—applications requiring version 1.0 might still require you to install that version separately. It all depends on exactly how the application was written.

A list of more specific new features, their impact, and the chapters in which they are discussed in more detail are shown in Table 1.2.

TABLE 1.2 Main Features of IIS 6

Feature	Impact	Chapter(s)
Application Health Monitoring	Improves the monitoring capabilities available to administrators for Web applications.	5
New Request Processor	Separates the IIS server component from the underlying OS and supporting applications, creating a more stable and secure platform that's less vulnerable to request-based attacks.	2, 5
Dynamic Content Caching	Enables content generated dynamically, which essentially doesn't change, to be cached by IIS for improved performance and lower CPU overhead.	5
ASP Template Caching	ASP templates are now stored on disk after processing from the ASP file, eliminating the need to recompile ASP templates that have expired from the in-memory cache.	5
Process Isolation	Enables the administrator to assign different applications to different execution pools; if an application fails or ties up the pool, other application pools continue to operate.	2, 5
ExecuteURL	Enables ISAPI filters to redirect requests to an alternative URL for processing.	6

TABLE 1.2   Main Features of IIS 6

Feature	Impact	Chapter(s)
Passport Integration	Enables Single Sign On (SSO) facilities for users with a valid Passport.	3
Low Privilege Execution	IIS now runs under a user with exceptionally low privileges, eliminating another potential weak point in security.	3
Lockdown mode	Shuts off all but the most basic static content— with dynamic content having to be specifically and individually enabled, which further reduces potential weak points.	3
XML Metabase	Enables for the easy modification and sharing of the configuration information stored in the metabase just by editing or copying the XML.	4
.NET Framework	Provides integration with the .NET system, including technologies such as Passport and dynamic systems, as well as languages supported by the .NET environment.	7
Improved Logging	IIS 6 can now log using UTF-8 (Unicode) text, useful for foreign language Web sites. A new binary mode makes for a more efficient and performance friendly method of logging compared to the text-base W3C format.	4
Granular Compression	Compression for responses can now be set at a more granular level, enabling compression on individual Web sites or folders instead of the whole server.	5
Quality of Service	Enables you to configure QoS parameters to prevent individual components of your Web site (IIS, dynamic content, and CPU/memory usage) by those components from affecting other sites and systems.	5

Availability

IIS 6 is a standard component of all versions of Windows Server 2003, but some of the additional components you can use with IIS and some of the more advanced functionality is only available in certain versions.

IIS 5.1 VS. 6.0

Although Windows Server 2003 is the server equivalent of Windows XP, Windows XP comes with IIS 5.1, an updated version of the original IIS 5 provided with Windows Server 2000.

Windows Server 2003 Family

Windows Server 2003 is essentially available in the same three core versions as Windows 2000—Standard Edition, Enterprise Edition, and Datacenter Edition. Windows Server 2003 also incorporates one version, Web Edition, specially designed for supporting Web sites and ideal for use in Web server farms.

 WEB RESOURCE

For more detail on Windows Server 2003, visit www.samspublishing.com and enter this book's ISBN number (no hyphens or parenthesis) in the Search field; then click the book cover image to access the book details page. Click the Web Resources link in the More Information section and locate article ID# **020102**.

Windows Server 2003, Standard Edition

The basic edition of Windows Server 2003 incorporates the main components required by the majority of users. It's ideally suited for low-demand application serving, but because of its limit of 4 CPUs, 4GB of RAM, and 4TB of disk space, it's unsuitable for higher-demand IIS applications.

Standard Edition is also limited only to Network Load Balancing in multiserver environments—with other clustering facilities only available in other editions.

If you intend to use only the Web serving capabilities, Web Edition will probably offer a more cost effective solution.

Windows Server 2003, Enterprise Edition

Enterprise Edition is designed to extend the reliability and scalability of the Standard Edition through a combination of extended hardware support and additional functionality.

Up to eight-way CPU systems can be used with Enterprise Edition, and it's the first version to support the 64-bit Itanium processor when it becomes available. This edition also increases the maximum RAM capability to 32GB. In addition, it supports Address Windows Extensions (AWE), which in a 4GB server can specifically reserve just 1GB for the core operating system, enabling the remaining 3GB to be used by applications. In the Standard and Web Editions, the addressable memory is split equally between the OS and applications.

Windows Clustering allows up to eight computers to be configured either for high performance, essentially using an extended form of the network load balancing technology, or as a high-availability setup, enabling automatic fail-over to a 'hot spare' machine in the event of a system failure.

The Enterprise Edition is unlikely to be used as an IIS platform largely because its main advantage over the Standard and Web Editions is the inclusion of clustering technology. Although clustering technology is useful, most Web sites and farms that require high availability and performance can achieve the same effect by using the Network Load Balancing features of the other editions.

However, this does not mean that the Enterprise Edition is not used in Web-based solutions. For sites that make use of either SQL Server or Exchange technologies, an Enterprise Edition server is likely to be in the background and it's mission critical when two or more servers will be configured in fail-over clustering mode.

Windows Server 2003, Datacenter Edition

You are unlikely to ever come across a server running Datacenter Edition. Unlike the other editions that are available separately for installation on the your own selection of hardware, Datacenter Edition is only available through some very select Datacenter partners.

These hardware manufacturers are responsible for supporting and providing the vital Hardware Abstraction Layer (HAL) for the Datacenter Edition. The hardware must also meet some very strict requirements and pass a battery of tests for compatibility and reliability before Microsoft will endorse the product. Once approved, the system can only use drivers signed and certified by Microsoft, and any hardware changes must also have been verified and passed the tests.

The result is a platform that is ultra reliable and specially designed both for high performance and high reliability. In fact, servers certified for the Datacenter program must achieve a 99.999% reliability, or about five minutes of unplanned downtime each year.

DATACENTER FOR HIGH AVAILABILITY

If Datacenter Edition is being used in a clustered setup, it's possible to achieve 100% availability, planned or unplanned, just by taking each individual server in a high-availability cluster out of service one at a time.

Therefore, Datacenter Edition is only available with the very high-end, top of the range and limits of current technology type hardware that you can normally only dream of. As a reflection of this, Datacenter Edition includes support for up to 64GB of RAM (256GB on Itanium) and 32 processors (64 on Itanium). Clustering support remains the same at 8 nodes per cluster.

As with the Enterprise Edition, it's highly unlikely that a Datacenter Edition machine will be used as a platform for IIS services, but it might be used to provide SQL Server or Exchange systems, or more likely clusters to support a Web application.

Windows Server 2003, Web Edition

If you look at the majority of machines that are used to support Web sites and applications today, you'll see that the vast majority of sites and companies are using a high number of relatively low-specification hardware. Often these units are 'pizza box' style; probably 1U high stacked into numerous 19 inch rack mount cupboards.

Physical limitations mean that these boxes are often limited to two processors and just 2GB of RAM. Coincidentally, this limitation also suits most strategies for providing high availability and performance Web sites. A large rack will take 42 1U high units: That's 42 dual-processor machines—all of which could be part of an NLB structure for handling thousands of Web site requests every second.

Microsoft has responded to this hardware-led approach by producing a version of Windows Server 2003 targeted squarely at this level of hardware with a comparable set of features specially designed for providing only Web-based services.

Windows Server 2003, Web Edition is therefore limited to supporting just 2GB of RAM and only two processors and without clustering technology, although it does include Network Load Balancing support.

The Web Edition also removes the need for the usual licensing restrictions. Because Web Edition doesn't allow anybody to actually connect directly to the machine—we have no file, print, or AD services to support—there is no need for either per connection or per seat licensing.

 WEB RESOURCE

For more information on how licensing and IIS operate, visit www.samspublishing.com and enter this book's ISBN number (no hyphens or parenthesis) in the Search field; then click the book cover image to access the book details page. Click the Web Resources link in the More Information section and locate article ID# **020103**.

In addition, Web Edition removes support for many of the features that a pure Web server just doesn't need, including

- Internet Authentication Services

- Internet Connection Sharing

- Internet Connection Firewall

- Network Bridging

- Removable Storage Management

- Fax Services

- Remote Installation Services

- Windows Media Services

- Services for Macintosh

Strangely, it also removes support for the Universal Data Definition Interface (UDDI) services, which are used to publish information on Web services. Web Edition is also only capable of being a member of an Active Directory domain; it cannot be a domain controller.

The result is a lighter, but more highly optimized and efficient, version of Windows Server 2003 designed especially for supporting Web applications.

The biggest benefit is probably the cost—almost a third of the price of the Standard Edition. Companies currently using Standard Edition in their rack mount systems will potentially save thousands of dollars each year.

Server Roles

Windows Server 2003 introduces some changes into the Windows server arena by giving administrators the power to assign their servers various different roles. These roles control the core feature set and available technologies installed and activated on the server. Although Windows 2000 included the concept of server roles, they were neither enforced nor easily available as configurable options. With Windows Server 2003, roles become a selectable component within the configuration of your Windows server.

For example, you can select the File Server role, which sets up the necessary services and systems on a server optimized for file serving, including the Windows and Mac file sharing systems, Distributed File System features, and Encrypted File System components. Other roles exist that automatically configure the server for print serving, terminal services, email, remote access, streaming media, WINS, domain controller, DNS server, and DHCP server

The Application Server role incorporates the various technologies designed for providing applications to other computers on a network. Because these typically consist of a Web component (including static content), various dynamic components such ASP pages, scripts, and database and other interfaces, the key technologies installed by selecting the Application Server role are

- Internet Information Server
- ASP
- ASP.NET
- COM+
- Microsoft Message Queuing (MSMQ)

The benefit of the role system is that it enables an administrator to set up a machine with only the components required to support the services he wants the machine to provide. With previous versions of Windows, you would need to install the operating system and then manually switch off components and services that you didn't need, such as file serving, print spoolers, and often many other components to optimize your server. The result is a more efficient and optimized server with lower installation and administration overheads.

Each server can have one or more roles, and you can configure the role setting in two places within Windows Server 2003. The primary location, and probably the easiest, is to use the Configure Your Server application. After the role has been selected and the software installed, you can manage the role and its capabilities through the Manage Your Server application.

Alternatively, you can manually install the components that make up different roles using the Add/Remove Components application. Using this method allows you to select the individual components and sub-components that you want to install, therefore giving you much finer control over the exact software installed on your system. For example, you could use this to install only IIS if your server were to be used only for static Web page serving.

Installing IIS

Over the years, Windows Server 2000 has had a number of different security problems. Although many of these have been internal problems, a large proportion—and many of the most public and embarrassing—have been directly attributable to IIS.

Part of the reason behind the problems, particularly when dealing with worms and viruses spread through IIS, has been that IIS is installed and enabled by default in all Windows 2000 installations. The moment you reboot after the installation has finished, IIS is running with a default series of security permissions, static elements, and some dynamic (and potentially lethal) elements.

It's often true that IIS is not the highest priority in many server installations. Although IIS is the primary Web server of choice on Windows, the majority of machines are used internally to provide directory, file, and print services, not as Web servers.

To help combat the problem, Microsoft has made IIS 6 an optional install and activate component rather than a default one. You enable and install IIS 6 by activating the Application Server role for your server after the initial installation.

Once enabled, IIS is in *Lockdown* mode, restricting the system to just basic static page serving. To enable more advanced features, including switching on ASP and ASP.NET extensions, you must separately configure IIS.

IIS LOCKDOWN MODE

Lockdown mode is a new security level defined by the new and improved security system built into both IIS and Windows Server 2003. I discuss Lockdown mode and other security options in Chapter 3, "Security."

To install IIS, perform the following steps:

1. Open Manage Your Server from the Start menu and click Add or Remove a Role.

2. You will be asked to attach any necessary peripherals before continuing. Click Next and wait while Windows checks your hardware.

3. In the list of server roles (as shown in Figure 1.1), click on Application Server. Click Next.

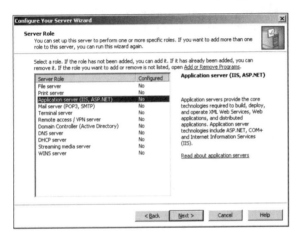

FIGURE 1.1 Selecting the Application Server role for your server.

4. If you want to enable FrontPage Server Extensions and ASP.NET, check the appropriate boxes. Click Next.

5. A summary of the operations to be carried out will appear (shown here in Figure 1.2). Click Next to start the installation.

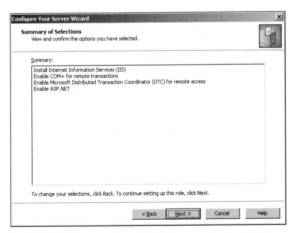

FIGURE 1.2 Checking the elements to be installed.

6. Windows will now install IIS and any additional components you selected. This can take a while. Be prepared to insert the installation CD-ROM if asked.

7. Click Finish to complete the configuration of your machine as an Application Server.

You should now be able to configure IIS using the IIS Manager that will have been installed in the Administrative Tools folder on the Start Menu.

Compatibility

Despite all the changes, at its heart, IIS 6 is still just a platform for serving Web pages. IIS 6 will still provide static pages to clients who ask for them, and many other core features—such as the support for CGI and scripting technologies, ASP, FrontPage extensions, and so on—remain the same.

In fact, unless you want to take advantage of many of the new features provided in IIS 6, you can continue to use IIS in the same way you have before using the IIS 5 Isolation mode. This makes IIS 6 work in a 100% compatible way with IIS 5, and anything that runs currently within IIS 5 should work identically when IIS 6 is operating in this mode.

IIS 5 Isolation mode is probably the easiest way to make a migration from a Windows 2000 hosted IIS 5 Web site to Windows Server 2003 while you get used to the new features and optimize and tune a server for use in native IIS 6 mode.

▶ For more information on making the migration from a previous version of IIS, see "Migrating from IIS 4/5 to IIS 6," (Chapter 7), **p.119**.

However, to make use of the new features, you will need to make some mental changes when working with the improved IIS snap-in for the Microsoft Management Console (MMC).

IIS 6 also includes a brand new Web-based interface for administration purposes, enabling you to monitor and manage your IIS installation even when MMC is not available.

Compatibility with most third-party filters, languages, and support tools is also retained. The ISAPI interface is still supported in IIS 6 and, in fact, includes a number of significant extensions, including the capability to 'chain' together ISAPI filters and to redirect requests from one URL to another location for processing.

However, it would be foolish not to take advantage of many of the new features, especially those specifically related to improving the stability and performance of your Web sites. If you are currently experiencing problems with crashed applications, hung services, and sometimes slow to respond servers, IIS 6 will eliminate many of the problems with few changes to your configuration.

▶ For more information on compatibility and migrating from IIS 4 (Windows NT) or IIS 5 (Windows 2000), refer to "Migrating from IIS 4/5 to IIS6," (Chapter 7), **p.119.**

Interestingly, IIS 6 is also the first IIS revision that closely matches the execution model of Apache. Apache is the most popular Web-serving platform on any operating system, but a number of people are already considering moving to Windows Server 2003 to take advantage of some of the more advanced integration and monitoring features.

▶ For more information on migrating your Apache installation to IIS 6, see "Migrating from Apache to IIS 6," (Chapter 8), **p.137**.

Architecture and Execution

What's New

The most fundamental change in IIS is the way it now processes requests from clients. In previous versions of IIS, a user-mode application was responsible for accepting requests and then sending them on to a separate application to be processed. This mode of operation severely limited both the performance of IIS and its stability because an external application could easily slow down or completely crash the IIS service. IIS 6 gets around this by moving the responsibility of accepting requests to the kernel and then providing protected memory spaces for individual Web applications.

Architecture

If you take a closer look at how previous versions of IIS have worked, you can see that IIS has always being trying to ice-skate uphill. The primary problem with IIS 5 and lower is that it was always a bolt-on attachment to the original operating system—although it was integrated into the security systems, operated as a service, and it was never truly an operating system component, such as the file service or active directory.

To add complications to this, the very nature of supporting Web applications means that you are immediately open to potential abuse from programmers and Web designers. Supporting most Web applications relies on using untrusted, third-party applications, often written by inexperienced programmers even when developing within a corporate environment.

The effect is to introduce a number of largely uncontrollable problems:

Stability—If an application supported through IIS crashes, the chances are that either it will crash IIS or it will 'steal' resources from other Web sites and applications.

Security—If the application provides a method for accessing the application in a nondocumented fashion, you have a potentially lethal security breach that could be used to access your entire network.

Performance—One top-heavy process has to deal the majority of the processing because a rogue user-mode application could be sapping CPU and memory from the other requests. Performance can be significantly impaired.

Scalability—Because a single process is responsible both for accepting and processing many of the requests, clients can be waiting to communicate a request while another user is still being serviced. When scaling up to multiple processors or machines, the same basic bottleneck remains.

Integration—Although previous versions gave the impression of being integrated into the OS, the reality is that IIS was just another application.

The solution within IIS 6 is to separate the two core stages in any HTTP request, the actual request and the response, and provide protected and independent areas for executing user sourced applications. This first component, the HTTP request mechanism, is supported by HTTP.sys—otherwise known as the Kernel Mode Driver. The second stage, the processing of the request and the response, is handled by a new system, called the application pool, which is in turn serviced by one or more worker processes.

 NOTHING NEW TO SEE?

If you're glancing at the Internet Services Manager and don't see any differences between IIS 5 and 6, it's because a lot is under the hood. This business of the kernel mode driver is a massive overhaul, and it truly makes IIS a part of the Windows OS now.

A second component, WWW Service Administration and Monitoring, then monitors both the kernel mode driver and the worker processes and enables you to monitor their status. It can also automatically reassign and manage the individual processes so that a failure in one application can be remedied without interrupting another request and without end users being aware of any problem.

These overall changes to the way in which IIS 6 handles requests have provided us with two different modes of operation—Worker Process Isolation Mode, the default, and IIS 5 Isolation Mode, a backward compatible mode most useful for migration. Both use similar components, but in different ways, so we'll look at each solution separately.

ONE MODE FOR EVERY SERVER

All the Web sites on each individual machine must run in the same mode. You *cannot* mix Worker Process and IIS 5 Isolation Modes on the same machine.

Worker Process Isolation Mode

To get a better idea of how the new architecture works, look at Figure 2.1. It shows how requests for information are processed.

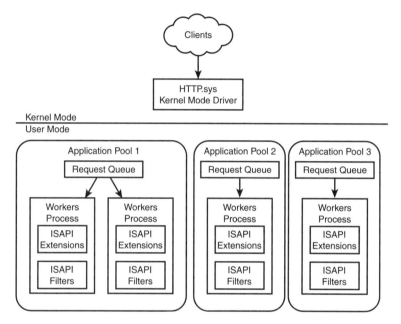

FIGURE 2.1   The HTTP.sys kernel mode driver marshals incoming requests before they are distributed to a suitable application pool.

▶ What I'm actually describing here is the default mode of operation, called Worker Process Isolation Mode. See "Worker Process Isolation Mode" this page for more information.

The HTTP.sys kernel mode driver waits for incoming requests. When a request from a client is received, one of two things happen:

- The request is handed off to the appropriate request queue within one of the configured application pools.

- The request is handled internally by the HTTP.sys driver for information that is cached when kernel mode caching has been switched on.

▶ See , "Performance and Reliability," (Chapter 5, **p. 97**) for more information on Kernel mode and other forms of caching.

Application pools are assigned to process requests for individual sites, URLs, or dynamically based on loading. For example, Figure 2.1 illustrates two application pools—Pool A could be configured to process queries for the URL http://www.mcslp.pri, whereas Pool B processes requests for http://admin.mcslp.pri.

By transferring the request to one of the queues, it immediately frees up the HTTP.sys driver to accept another request from a client and process it accordingly. The bottleneck from the old request processor, which did both jobs, has been eliminated by making the primary point of contact merely a marshaling tool. This increases the number of requests that can be processed by the server without requiring any physical improvements to the machine, just through better management of the requests themselves.

Each application pool is in charge of a number of worker processes. These processes in turn handle the authentication and authorization and ultimately execute the underlying ISAPI filter or application to process the next request from the queue. Application pools work independently of each other, and worker processes within a pool work independently of each other, as well.

We'll look at each component in more detail so you can understand the underlying configuration and administration requirements for each section.

HTTP.sys (Kernel Mode Driver)

HTTP.sys is a kernel level driver, and it's responsible for just one thing—listening for incoming requests on a given IP address and port for incoming HTTP queries. After the request has been accepted, it's placed into the appropriate request queue, and HTTP.sys returns to process the next request.

HTTP.SYS IS JUST FOR HTTP

Other TCP/IP services are still handled by InetInfo.exe; only HTTP requests are handled by HTTP.sys.

The basic premise of HTTP.sys is to accept and process the incoming request from a client as quickly as possible to achieve the highest possible client connection acceptance rate. In standard operation, that means handing off the connection to the appropriate application pool. But if kernel mode caching has been enabled, the data is returned directly to the client without any further disk access or application execution.

Because HTTP.sys operates at the kernel level, it has a higher priority than most user-mode processes and it has direct access to the TCP/IP driver stack. Also, as a kernel driver, it is incapable of processing user-level code, thus making it impossible for any user-level code, such as that used by one of the assigned application pools, to cause the primary point of client contact to fail or stop accepting requests.

HTTP.SYS AND IIS

If we want to be strictly correct, HTTP.sys is in fact not part of IIS at all: It merely provides a facility within the kernel that allows IIS to function. IIS is built on top of HTTP.sys and the rest of the kernel. That said, without HTTP.sys, IIS wouldn't work.

 ## HTTP.SYS IS A GENERIC SERVICE

Because HTTP.sys is just a marshaling service for requests, it's possible to build other responders on top of the HTTP.sys service to augment or even replace the functionality of IIS. Although not, perhaps, to everyone's liking, it would be possible to put Apache in place of IIS as the request processing service; however, it would still receive the actual requests from HTTP.sys.

HTTP.sys is also responsible for all text-based logging for the WWW service. Because it is the primary contact point, it is the obvious choice and it enables IIS to log requests as soon as they have been received without having to wait for the response from the corresponding user application.

▶ For more information on the logging parameters and new log features in IIS 6, see "Management and Monitoring," (Chapter 4), **p.65**.

Finally, HTTP.sys is responsible for implementing the Quality of Service (QoS) functionality, which controls the core connectivity parameters, such as connection limits, timeouts, queue lengths, and bandwidth throttling.

▶ For more information on the Quality of Service system, see (Chapter 5) **p. 104**.

HTTP.SYS AND SSL

The kernel mode driver HTTP.sys is incapable of decrypting or encrypting SSL requests. Instead, a separate filter is applied at the user-mode level to decrypt the incoming request before passing it off to the corresponding application pool.

Application Pools

The application pool is a highly configurable element of the user-mode component of servicing HTTP requests. Each application pool consists of one request queue, which holds the incoming client requests passed on by HTTP.sys, and one (or more) worker process that services those requests.

Each application pool is separated from other pools through the use of a separate process for each pool. Application pools are handled in user mode, naturally separating them from the kernel mode driver HTTP.sys and also making them more easily configurable and manageable.

Individual applications can be assigned to a single application pool, and one application pool can service the requests of multiple applications. However, you cannot assign a single application to use more than one application pool—to improve performance, you instead increase the number of worker processes servicing the requests.

Application pools, like the rest of the system, are monitored, and it's possible to configure individual pools to handle their worker processes in a number of different ways. For example, you can configure one application pool to continually renew each worker process after a set number of requests or perhaps after a set period of time.

This particular model of application pools improves on the original concept of isolation introduced in IIS 4 and builds on the application namespace solution in IIS 5. The overall effect provides the following benefits:

Clean separation between the user and kernel code—It's now impossible for a derived application to bring down the entire IIS service. Instead, either only the application pool will be brought down, or more likely, the worker process causing the problem will be restarted by the monitoring service.

Multiple application pools—They make it much easier and efficient to host multiple sites on a single server. For companies (particularly ISPs) that support a number of clients on a single server, you can configure separate pools on a per-client or even per-site basis without fear of upsetting other client's hosting stability.

Worker process management—Worker processes are monitored and managed so that it's impossible for a worker process to halt the entire server. You can configure an application pool only to create a worker process when it's required by the application pool, reducing long-term resource use—ideal for low traffic sites or those that are used only at specific times. Furthermore, a timeout can be set when the process will be terminated if it hasn't been used.

Rapid-fail protection—If the worker processes in an application continually fail, the WWW service can take the application out of service, reporting error 503 (Service unavailable) to further client requests.

Load balancing support—The application pool concept works perfectly with load balancing technologies. Now it's possible to distribute requests within the same server with the same level of application separation that was previously only available across a number of machines.

Request Queues

The request queue handles the incoming requests supplied by HTTP.sys waiting to be processed by the corresponding application pool. One request queue exists for each pool. However, the request queue is not a marshaling service as such; it just provides a place for requests to be queued. It is the responsibility of individual worker processes to apply for requests from the queue to work on.

Worker Processes

Worker processes answer individual requests as part of an application pool. Each worker process, an instance of the W3wp.exe application, runs in user mode and is therefore separately manageable and monitored by the WWW Service administration and monitoring component.

Worker processes are solely responsible for invoking an ISAPI filter (including ASP and ASP.NET) or running a CGI handler when working with CGI-based applications.

Individual worker processes also handle authentication and authorization, and this ties in with the default authorization level of the worker process applications. By default, worker processes run as NetworkService, which has the strongest security (and therefore the least default access).

Because worker processes operate independently of the system that accepts the requests from the client, we can manage and control the worker processes to solve performance and reliability problems. Through the application pools, we can also control the availability, responsiveness, and performance of individual applications.

In fact, worker processes are highly configurable. Here are some of the main elements that can be tuned and their benefits:

Health monitoring—We can monitor individual worker processes, creating, killing, and restarting them according to the settings of the application pool—improving stability and freeing up resources when worker processes are not required.

Processor affinity—You can assign individual worker processes to specific processors within an SMP system, either to make the best use of the available processor resource or to take advantage of better L1 or L2 caching in each processor. Such fine control can make a real performance difference with some applications.

CPU monitoring—Individual worker processes can be limited to specific amounts of CPU time, allowing you to efficiently distribute your CPU time between application pools, worker processes, and, ultimately, clients.

Demand start—The monitoring system can dynamically create a worker process when the application pool receives a request. By not permanently keeping worker processes running, the resources can be used by other applications and processes in the system.

Idle timeout—Linked to the *Demand Start* feature, we can also kill off worker processes that identify themselves as idle, freeing up those vital resources.

Orphan control—If the WWW monitoring service identifies a worker process that is causing serious problems, but not necessarily dead or failed, it can either kill or orphan the process. This involves killing and then restarting the worker process to prevent its state affecting the operation of the pool. When orphaning is enabled, the killed process continues to execute, but a new process is started to handle requests. You can also configure orphans to be automatically debugged.

Manual recycling—To prevent worker processes from 'going stale,' eating up resources, or for those applications suffering from hard to identify problems, individual worker processes can be recycled (killed and recreated). This can be done without affecting the availability of the Web site.

Automatic recycling (restarting)—As an extension of the manual recycling, worker processes can also be automatically recycled based on

- Elapsed time

- Number of requests served

- Scheduled time within a 24-hour period

- Result of a 'liveliness ping'

- Virtual Memory usage

- Physical Memory usage

As with the manual process, this recycling happens in the background without affecting the execution or availability of the site. HTTP.sys will continue to accept and queue requests, and those requests waiting in the queue will be processed as soon as a worker process becomes available.

WEB GARDENS

If you configure multiple worker processes within a single application pool, IIS 6 operates as a Web garden—similar to the larger, multiple machine Web farms and retaining many of the benefits.

First and foremost, the stability of your site can be enhanced. If one request is taking a particularly long time or the application crashes, other worker processes in the garden can continue to handle requests.

On multiprocessor machines, a multi-worker process application pool will execute Web applications much more efficiently by distributing and executing multiple requests simultaneously.

WWW Service Administration and Monitoring Component

By now it should be clear that the WWW Service Administration and Monitoring Component (WSAMC) provides a critical part of the overall system. The WSAMC component handles two main areas—configuration and process management.

When IIS 6 starts, the request process manager portion of the WSAMC, which is responsible for distributing requests, loads the IIS metabase. The WSAMC then creates the routing table, which associates a specific URL with one of the configured application pools, and this is used to redirect requests received through HTTP.sys.

Then, the WSAMC system notifies HTTP.sys of the different request queues and routing parameters that ultimately enable the Web service. Changes to the metabase, either directly or through the IIS MMC snap-in, update the routing table, and HTTP.sys is updated with the changes.

When the system is up and running, the request processor in the WSAMC is responsible for managing the individual worker processes, including starting, stopping, and recycling processes, as well as also monitoring and recycling those processes that have failed if necessary.

Web Application Isolation

As the name suggests, the idea of Worker Process Isolation mode is to isolate user-mode operations into one or more application pools and in turn, one or more worker processes—all completely separate and also separate from the primary contact point, HTTP.sys.

You can see this isolation more clearly if you refer back to Figure 2.1. Application Pools 2 and 3 are single worker process pools, whereas Pool 1 is a Web garden pool. A failure in Pool 2 will not affect the other two pools. More importantly, it's unlikely that a failure in a single worker process in Pool 1 would have a significant affect on the other worker processes.

Because of this isolation, when IIS 6 works in this mode, you get an effective combination of stability and performance. The stability comes from the way in which we can individually control each application pool and worker process, including the monitoring and automatic recycling of failed processes.

The performance improvements are introduced through the use of separate worker processes and application pools. Within the pools, we can tune the parameters to give specific response time and execution parameters. Using multiple worker processes, we can also spread the load of requests over one or more processes and ultimately individual processors, making use of SMP technology.

IIS 5 Isolation Mode

IIS 5 Isolation Mode was designed to retain compatibility with applications that are currently being supported under IIS 5 on Windows 2000. Unfortunately, this mode eliminates many of the features in worker process isolation mode, including application pools, worker processes, recycling, and the health monitoring features.

What doesn't change is the role of HTTP.sys as a kernel-level component for accepting requests from clients. You can see the model for this mode in Figure 2.2. The request model in this mode matches, almost identically, the request path of IIS 5.

You can see here that HTTP.sys handles the requests, but all requests are appended to the same, global request queue, which is used by all the other components and applications. There are no individual queues, and no way to configure requests at an individual application level.

The requests are handled by the WWW service, with Inetinfo.exe, the same application used in IIS 5/Windows 2000, handling the static requests and providing the execution environment for integrated ISAPI filters and extensions used in low-isolation Web applications.

Medium (pooled) and high-level applications are still handled with separate, out of process, application hosts through the DLLHost.exe application.

 UPGRADING AND COMPATIBILITY

If you're upgrading from Windows 2000 and IIS 5, leave IIS 6 set to function in IIS 5 Isolation Mode to start with. If you've installed Windows Server 2003 as an upgrade, rather than as a new installation, this will be how it is configured anyway. You'll be assured of your Web applications continuing to work until you've had a chance to thoroughly test them under IIS 6's native modes.

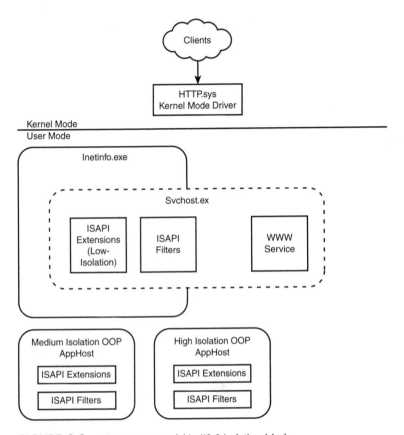

FIGURE 2.2   The request model in IIS 5 Isolation Mode.

Web Application Isolation

IIS 5 Isolation Mode offers three different isolation modes for individual applications supported by IIS. These are similar to the modes in IIS 5:

> **Low (IIS Process)** applications run 'in-process' within the Inetinfo.exe application and are not protected from other applications that are also running in-process. Applications execute using the default identity **LocalSystem**.

> **Medium (Pooled)** applications run as DLLs within a single DLLHost.exe instance. These applications are protected from the effects of failures in both high and low applications, but not from failures from other applications in the same pool. Applications execute by default as **IWAM_ComputerName**.

> **High (Isolated)** applications run as DLLS in DLLHost.exe and are both isolated from other applications, and other applications are isolated from them. Applications execute by default as **IWAM_ComputerName**.

Isolation Mode Comparison

You can quickly identify the main differences between the two application modes and which application services requests using Table 2.1. Note that because worker processes are responsible for running all ISAPI components, there is no such thing as an out-of-process ISAPI extension.

TABLE 2.1 Comparing IIS 5 and Worker Process Isolation Modes

	IIS 5 Isolation Mode		Worker Process Isolation Mode	
IIS Function	**Component**	**Application**	**Component**	**Application**
Worker processes	N/A	N/A	WWW Service	Svchost.exe
Worker process management	N/A	N/A	Worker process	W3wp.exe
In-process ISAPI extensions		Inetinfo.exe	Worker process	W3wp.exe
Out-of-process ISAPI extensions		DLLHost.exe	(none)	(none)
ISAPI Filters		Inetinfo.exe	Worker process	W3wp.exe
HTTP.sys Config	WWW Service	Svchost.exe	WWW Service	Svchost.exe
HTTP Protocol	Windows kernel	HTTP.sys	Windows kernel	HTTP.sys
IIS Metabase		Inetinfo.exe		Inetinfo.exe
Authentication		lsass.exe	Worker process	W3wp.exe/lsass.exe
SSL		Inetinfo.exe		lsass.exe
FTP		Inetinfo.exe		Inetinfo.exe
NNTP		Inetinfo.exe		Inetinfo.exe
SMTP		Inetinfo.exe		Inetinfo.exe

Default Settings

Depending on how you have installed Windows Server 2003 and IIS 6, the system will have automatically determined the default operation mode of your IIS 6 installation. Table 2.2 illustrates a quick overview.

TABLE 2.2 Default Operating Modes for Different Installation Types

Installation	**Default Isolation Mode**
New Installation	Worker process isolation mode
Upgrade from previous IIS 6 version	No change from previous mode
Upgrade from Windows 2000/IIS 5	IIS 5 Isolation Mode
Upgrade from Windows NT/IIS 4	IIS 5 Isolation Mode

Configuration

Although they've been portrayed here as separate components, HTTP.sys, applications pools, and worker process are all configured through the same basic set of interfaces within the IIS management snap-in for the MMC.

The majority of the configurable settings available to you for IIS 6's core architecture are useful only when working in Worker Process Isolation Mode. Unless otherwise noted, all the configurable options in this section relate to using IIS 6 in this mode.

▶ For information on configuring the IIS 5 Isolation Mode, see the "Switching to IIS 5 Isolation Mode" section, **p.38**.

▶ Many of the application pool parameters will affect the performance of your Web sites, and many will either affect or occasionally directly contradict the effects of another setting. For information on monitoring IIS and then tuning the various parameters, including their interactions, see (Chapter 5) **p.97**.

Application Pool Management

Application pools are configured directly within the IIS snap-in of MMC. You can see the default IIS configuration panel, with a number of sites and application pools already configured, in Figure 2.3.

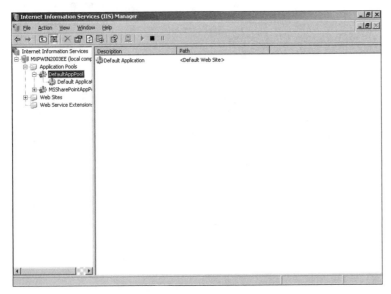

FIGURE 2.3   Application pools on a typical Web server.

Creating and Naming Application Pools

To create a new pool, right-click on the Application Pools folder and select **New, Application Pool**. You'll see the dialog box in Figure 2.4.

FIGURE 2.4   Setting up a new application pool.

You need to enter the application pool ID—just a name to identify the pool. You can opt either to use the default settings or to copy the settings from an existing pool.

Once created, the new pool appears in the list of available application pools in the IIS browser. The majority of the configurable parameters within each pool apply either to the request queue component or to the management of worker processes; we'll look at those elements individually.

Using Templates

If you are setting up a number of application pools, you can use predefined templates in one of two ways. Either select the name of an existing application pool whose settings will be copied, or you can save your application pool settings to a file and use the file to generate new application pools. The latter method has the benefit that you can create application pool types without having to actually activate a particular pool for use as a template.

To save an application pool template to a file, create a new application pool in the standard way, right-click on the pool, and then select **All Tasks, Save Configuration to a File**. You will be prompted for a filename and a path in which to save the file. You can also optionally encrypt the configuration by entering a password.

ENCRYPTING CONFIGURATIONS
Encrypted configurations are useful if you want to create complex, high-performance templates that can only then be installed by specific administrators.

To create a new application from a template file, right-click on an application and select **New, Application pool (from file)**. You will be prompted for a filename, or you can browse to a directory of existing configurations and select your choice from a list.

EASIER IDENTIFICATION

Use a descriptive name for the file in which you save your configuration to make it easy to identify later. You might want to accept a standard description format that orders things accordingly—for example, always specifying whether a pool template uses Web gardens or recycling.

Allocating Sites to Pools

Application pool allocation works in a similar fashion to the Application setting within IIS 5. To set a specific application to a specific pool, perform the following steps:

1. Open the root properties for the application you want to manage.

2. Go to the Directory, Home Directory, or the Virtual Directory tab (see Figure 2.5).

FIGURE 2.5   Selecting an application pool for a Web site.

3. For directory or virtual directory sites, ensure that you have given the application a name.

4. Choose the application pool to use from the Application pool pop-up.

5. Click OK.

 NOT NECESSARILY PLUG AND PLAY

If you thought IIS was just an install-and-forget-it thing, think again. Web applications deserve your attention, and taking the time to configure application pools will pay off in performance benefits.

Starting and Stopping Pools

You can start, stop, or recycle an entire application pool by using the options in the drop-down menu when you right-click on the pool you want to manage:

Start will start a currently stopped pool.

Stop will stop a currently running pool, enabling all applications that use this pool.

Recycle will shut down and then restart all the worker processes within the pool.

Remember that stopping an application pool will stop processing of all requests for an application that uses that pool. If you are having persistent problems with a particular application or pool, use the monitoring and recycling features to manage the application pool automatically.

Request Queue Parameters

Only one configurable parameter exists for the request queue component, and it is found under the Performance tab of the properties for an application pool.

If selected (it's on by default), the Request Queue Limit allows you to specify the number of requests that will be queued. When the queue is full, the application will respond with the HTTP error 503 (Server Unavailable) to clients.

If you don't set this option, or you set the number of requests to accept too high, a potentially unlimited number of requests could bog down your application pool and ultimately your server, bringing it to a grinding halt, irrespective of what other settings you have in place.

Set the value too low, and you risk locking out users from your server when it potentially isn't even busy.

The value you set depends entirely on what applications the pool is servicing and what your expected response times are. The aim is to keep your request at a level that never enables the pool to reach your desired maximum request time. For example, if you set a target of a five second response, you should set a limit that processes a full queue within that period.

For some hints on some typical values for different situations, see Table 2.3. Although I've given specific figures, ideally you should really compare the relative sizes between applications. Keep in mind that different applications will imply different processing times and therefore request queue sizes.

TABLE 2.3 Sample Settings for the Request Queue Length

Site Type	Queue Setting	Discussion
Static Pages	1000–2000	With static pages, the server is really only reading a file off the disk and sending the data back to the client. This is a relatively light duty, so it takes little time to process. On a fast server, particularly one with two or more CPUs and employing multiple worker processes, you might be able to increase the values still further.
Built-in/Embedded ISAPI Filters	500–1000	These have a slightly larger load because additional code and applications will be required to process the requests. The ideal setting is highly application specific.
ASP/ASP.NET	250–500	ASP/ASP.NET implies a relatively high CPU requirement over static page provision, and therefore the value reflects this increased processing time. For simple applications, especially when using ASP for templating with the template caching option enabled, you could increase this to a value similar to that of the static pages. For solutions that process Web requests or provide interfaces to databases, keep in mind that the request time must include the time to process the DB request, as well as process the data and return the desired HTML.
CGI-based applications	125–250	Most CGI applications require the loading of an external process for the request to be processed. Starting a new application is one of the most intensive operations and so the load is significantly higher than an ISAPI based process.

 WEB RESOURCE

For more information on the various performance parameters within IIS 6, visit www.samspub-lishing.com and enter this book's ISBN number (no hyphens or parenthesis) in the Search field; then click the book cover image to access the book details page. Click the Web Resources link in the More Information section and locate article ID# **020201**.

Worker Process Parameters

You can configure the number of worker processes started by an application pool using the Web garden settings in the Performance tab of the pool's properties. The default for a new pool is to use only one worker process.

The exact setting of this parameter depends on a combination of the underlying hardware, the loading effects of your application, and the total number of application pools configured in your system. In general, it's not recommended to have more than one worker process per CPU for each configured application pool.

Performance Parameters

The Performance tab, shown in Figure 2.6, configures the core performance settings for your application pool. I've already covered the request queue and Web garden parameters separately; the other two settings control the idle timeout and CPU loading.

FIGURE 2.6   Performance parameters for an application pool.

CPU Loading

It's possible to limit the amount of CPU used by an application pool. Throttling the application pools in this way can be useful if you are mixing customers who have different site response time requirements, or if you are hosting a number of sites over a number of individual pools and want to avoid one pool absorbing all the available resources.

This setting is similar to the process throttling setting in IIS 5, but is more configurable and works on an application pool rather than a Web site basis. By controlling individual pools in this manner, you can set up a number of specific pools—for example, four pools with 5%, 15%, 25%, and 55% throttling and redistribute groups of sites according to needs.

In addition to setting the maximum CPU usage for the pool, you can also configure the period over which the usage is monitored. (The default is five minutes.)

As with IIS 5, we can also control what happens when the limit is reached. The available actions are the same as under IIS 5:

No action—Nothing happens except the logging of the event. This is equivalent to leaving the Enforce Limits unchecked under IIS 5.

Shutdown—All worker processes within the application pool are marked for termination and allowed to shut down within the Shutdown Time parameter limits. This is equivalent to checking the Enforce Limits box under IIS 5.

Idle Timeout

Worker processes require tiny amounts of processor time and memory even when they are not actually processing requests. On a server that hosts a number of low-volume Web sites, the potential exists to create hundreds or thousands of worker processes that are doing nothing, reducing the server's capability to service other requests.

Using this parameter, IIS will monitor inactive worker processes and shut down those that have been idle for the specified period. The default is 90 seconds. As soon as a request is made to the application pool, a new worker process is started.

Obviously, starting a new process has an implied overhead, so you don't want to have worker processes always having to be started automatically through this system because this will slow your response times.

You might want to lower the shutdown time period in the following situations:

- Sites that have low-traffic volumes, but occasional high bursts for short periods (for example, a report generation system run once a month)

- On servers that have a high number of low-volume sites where you have created one pool per customer

- Sites that have sporadic access but overall low volume

You might want to increase the time period when you have

- A relatively busy site with occasional dips in usage

- A low volume, but regular usage site

Health Monitoring Parameters

The health monitoring features of an application control how the pool responds to problems with individual worker processes. The aim of tuning these parameters is to provide a balance between worker process availability and keeping idle worker processes to a minimum.

You can see an example of the Health tab in Figure 2.7.

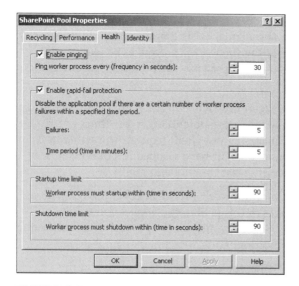

FIGURE 2.7 Automatically monitoring the health of your application pools.

▶ Chapter 5 (**p.97**) contains further information on tuning these parameters for optimum processing.

Enable Pinging

If you enable this setting, individual worker processes will be tested to verify their responsiveness. If the worker process fails to respond, the worker process is recycled, killing the failed process and re-creating a replacement. You can specify the delay period (the default is 30 seconds) between each ping using the box provided.

You should change this setting with care because it has the potential to kill perfectly healthy worker processes if set incorrectly. Setting too low a value might cause the system to recycle a process that is simply busy processing a request. Setting too high a value could leave a crashed process running. In a single worker process environment, this could stop your Web site completely. Even in Web garden installations, the crashed process could present a serious performance hit.

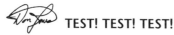 **TEST! TEST! TEST!**

Be sure to thoroughly test your applications and your worker process settings, especially the ping settings. You don't want to modify these settings on a production server and find out that you made a bad choice!

Enable Rapid-Fail Protection

Because worker processes execute user code, the potential exists that a problem in the user application could cause continual failures, requiring the worker process to be re-created. Unless you were continually checking this, you would probably never notice, but the effects of the problem are two-fold.

First, your system becomes excessively busy without ever achieving anything because the load of starting a new worker process each time one fails—potentially many times every second on a busy site—is quite high. Second, many of your client requests will either be processed, terminated in mid-response, or your site might have stopped responding altogether. It will be impossible, as a client, to identify what the problem might be.

To help resolve this, rapid-fail protection will monitor worker processes over a given period, and if the processes fail a set of number of times in this period, the application will be disabled, causing HTTP.sys to return a 403 (service not available) error rather than continuing to service requests for an obviously faulty application.

There are two settings—the time period over which the checks will take place and the number of failures that have to be registered within that period. Setting these limits needs careful consideration:

- Setting too high a failure rate within a short period of time is unlikely to trigger protection because there is a finite failure/recycle rate for worker processes.

- Setting too low a failure rate within a long period might also never trigger protection.

As with other parameters, the settings need to be tuned both according to the application and with the expected response time of the application in mind. To put this into context, if it takes 10 seconds to process a request, setting parameters of 30 failures in 5 minutes is impractical.

Instead, work on a percentage failure rate—for example, you might want to trigger protection if the failures exceed 10% of requests at typical load within a 5 minute period. In this instance, a setting of 3 failures within 5 minutes would be appropriate.

Startup and Shutdown Time Limits

When worker processes are recycled, or after being identified as unhealthy, they are not terminated immediately. Instead, the process is marked for termination and given a grace period to complete the processing of any outstanding requests.

The *Shutdown time limit* parameter defines the duration of the grace period. The time limit needs to be set carefully so that you do not terminate execution before any outstanding requests have been processed. For example, for an application that has an average response time of 10 seconds, you should set a figure below 30 seconds to avoid terminating in-progress applications.

The *Startup time limit* defines the period in which a new worker process must start before it should be ready for handling requests. Failure to startup within a given time frame will be recorded and if necessary used in the rapid fail protection system to prevent an application from starting up in an unstable condition.

Identity Parameters

All worker processes within a given application pool are executed as the same user. You can configure which user this is using the Identity tab of the application pool properties.

The default user is the *Network Service* account, which has the least user rights, required to execute Web applications. It's therefore the safest user to use because it provides the least number of opportunities for a cracker to gain access to your system.

Other selectable options are

> **Local Service**—Similar to Network Service, but with rights only for the current machine.
>
> **Local System**—The least secure option, this user gives almost unlimited access to the host system. Do not use unless you are either using a test system *not* connected to your internal network, or use sparingly with applications that use both SSL and some form of authentication.

Alternatively, you can use any user on the system providing you supply his username and password. Note that any user you choose should be a member of the IIS_WPG group; otherwise, the application pool will fail.

▶ For more information on the different users for use with IIS and their abilities, see "Security," (Chapter 3), **p.39**.

Depending on your configuration, you might want to use the default Network Service account. The primary reason for using an alternative account is to compartmentalize individual users.

Recycling Parameters

Often, even with a well-behaved application, the potential exists for the application to start using more resources than it should. Sometimes, you might even have applications that either you cannot fix or cannot identify the problem that needs to be fixed.

> **STATIC CONTENT DOESN'T RECYCLE**
> If you are only serving static content that does not require ISAPI extensions or filters, you shouldn't need to use the recycling system.

Previously with IIS 5, you'd either have to manually monitor the system or alternatively use IISReset or a VB, Perl, or other application to periodically stop and restart the Web service. In either case, you run the risk of disabling all of your sites from your potential visitors during the cycle.

In IIS 6, the capability to schedule a recycle of the worker processes handling requests for an application pool is built in. Because of the changes to the request system and application isolation, individual worker processes can be restarted without affecting the availability of individual sites or applications, or the IIS system as a whole.

The recycling system recycles worker processes in one of two ways:

> In low-load conditions, where very few requests are being handled by the application pool, the existing worker process will be terminated and a new one started in its place.

> In all other situations (and indeed the default configuration), a new worker process is to be started while the existing process still processes requests; when the new worker process is ready, the new one takes over and the old one is terminated.

Using this approach keeps the application pool busy servicing requests without losing any availability—there's no period of time when a given pool is unable to service requests.

Worker processes are configured through the Recycling tab of the application properties window. You can recycle parameters according to a number of different settings. If you specify more than one setting, the settings are combined—with processes recycled by whichever method triggers the recycle process first.

For example, if you recycle by request and duration, the recycling will be triggered if the process reaches the request limit before the duration expires, or if the duration expires before the request limit is reached. After a worker process has been restarted, all counters are reset, irrespective of the trigger.

MONITORING PROCESS RECYCLING

You can monitor when worker processes are recycled automatically by setting the LogEventOnRecycle property within the IIS Metabase. Suitable entries will then be made in WWW Service log.

Regular Time Period

Worker processes can be automatically recycled after they have been executing for the specified number of minutes using the Recycle Worker Processes (in Minutes) setting. If you use this setting with a Web garden, the restarting of individual processes is staggered to retain uptime, but all processes in the application will be restarted within the given time frame.

The duration setting is the most practical of the settings in situations where you suspect a problem that is non-fatal or not serious enough to warrant strict checking. If you are having an intermittent problem, use this setting in combination with the health monitoring parameters so that you can both pre-empt and recover from potential problems.

Regular Request Period

The regular request period setting—Recycle worker processes (number of requests)—triggers recycling when a worker process has handled the specified number of requests. For example, setting a value to 500 would automatically restart the worker process after it has handled 500 requests.

This setting is best used with applications where you know it has a specific problem, perhaps a memory leak, that manifests itself at a particular execution limit. For example, an application that gradually eats RAM could be set to recycle before it uses too much. You might also want to consider the Memory Recycling settings.

Specific Times

If your Web site has well-defined usage and you have known gaps or deliberate administration downtimes, you can set the recycling to occur at specific times. To use this setting, first click the check box, and then click Add to specify a particular time. Existing times can be removed using Delete, and you can modify an entry using Edit.

As with the duration setting and Web gardens, worker processes are not recycled simultaneously, but instead staggered around the times you specify to prevent the application pool from failing to handle a request.

Memory Recycling

User applications with problems frequently exhibit memory leaks, which use virtual and physical memory that could otherwise be allocated to other worker processes. These are finite resources, so it's a good idea to protect their usage by enabling these settings.

Unlike the other settings, the memory settings apply to individual worker processes within a given application. If one worker process reaches the specific limits, it's the only process that is recycled; other processes will continue to execute as normal. This makes these settings ideal for controlling memory usage if all the other problems with an application do not affect execution.

Be very careful with these settings, however. Some applications can genuinely require large amounts of memory—for example, database applications that generate large queries. Setting the values too low could increase the load on the system by generating too many recycling triggers. Conversely, setting the figures too high can mean that the recycle is never triggered, even though the effects could be having a detrimental affect on your system.

You can tune these parameters through careful monitoring of the worker process memory size and your available virtual and physical memory. Alternatively, try to avoid using more than 50% of either setting across all your application pools. For example, with 4GB of virtual memory and two application pools, you would set a limit of 1GB on each pool before a recycle is triggered.

WEB RESOURCE

For more information on Memory and DLL Management in IIS 5, visit
www.samspublishing.com and enter this book's ISBN number (no hyphens or parenthesis) in
the Search field; then click the book cover image to access the book details page. Click the Web
Resources link in the More Information section and locate article ID# **020202**.

Switching to IIS 5 Isolation Mode

If you want to change your server to run Web sites using IIS 5 Isolation Mode, implement the
following steps:

1. Open the Properties dialog box for all Web Sites within your server.

2. Click the Service tab.

3. Select Run WWW Service in IIS 5.0 Isolation Mode.

4. Click OK.

5. You will be prompted to accept the change. Click Yes to continue.

ISOLATION MODE DISABLES WORKER PROCESSES!
This will disable worker process isolation mode because the two modes cannot co-exist.
Any existing requests will be completed before the change takes place; although it won't
interrupt existing requests, new requests might have to wait until the existing requests
have completed successfully.

From then on, most parameters work as they did in IIS 5. For example, to configure application isolation modes, you use the Application Protection setting in the directory, home, or
virtual directory tab of the Web site's properties.

Most significant of the parameters that disappear from IIS 5 Isolation Mode is the CPU throttling parameter. There is no way to configure this setting when the machine is in IIS 5
Isolation Mode.

The option to configure individual application pools in your system will disappear. In fact,
you won't even be able to select an application pool. Your settings will be retained though, so
if you disable IIS 5 Isolation Mode, your application pools and their configurations will
return.

Security

What's New

IIS has a rather unfortunate reputation of being relatively insecure. This is largely due to a number of relatively high-profile attacks on the IIS platform. In recent years, the most famous of these was the NIMDA worm and the Code Red worm before it, which spread through a vulnerability in the IIS code.

The worm spread very quickly for two reasons. First, IIS was installed and enabled by default on Windows 2000, and was a frequently installed component of Windows NT 4.0 through the Option Pack even if IIS wasn't required. This meant that in many cases, computers that weren't even acting as IIS servers were exploitable. Because it was already installed, many administrators never disabled it and never considered it a threat.

The second problem is more difficult to counter. It's impossible to preconceive every possible attack, and frequently the exploits used by the hackers are either impossible to predict bugs or deliberate attempts to overload the application to the point where the excess of information crosses a crack through which the code enters.

Outside the realm of malicious attempts to break in to your IIS installation, the general security of your machine and Web sites is fairly high. Preventing your users from accidentally finding their way into a secure part of the site is handled through a number of security systems, including both authentication—that is, identifying the user—and authorization—the access rights and restrictions placed on different files, folders, and Web sites according to a user's credentials.

Microsoft has worked hard with IIS 6 to produce a secure environment, countering the potential gaps and problems by denying access or ability to a visiting user unless that feature or area has been specifically enabled by the administrator.

At the most fundamental level, they achieved this by not installing IIS by default. All Windows Server 2003 computers must specifically be enabled with IIS functionality through the Server Roles Wizard. Even when installed, IIS only serves static content, with dynamic processing tools such as ASP disabled, so it isn't possible for ASP or other code to execute on your Web server unless you've specifically allowed it.

Again, even when ASP is enabled, IIS is still in a relatively safe position—because, by default, all worker processes execute using a low privilege account. This prevents malicious ASPs from having access to the various parts of your system, and it also prevents non-malicious scripts from accidentally overwriting or modifying files they shouldn't have access too.

Further improvements in the security of IIS at an application level are offered through an expanded set of authentication methods, including integration with Microsoft's Passport system and improvements to the Secure Sockets Layer (SSL) implementation.

Behind the scenes, outside the direct scope of IIS, there are also some changes to the way the OS operates. Most notably, we can now control and limit the availability of IIS through group policy, allowing you to specify at a domain or OU level which machines can install IIS.

 WEB RESOURCE

For a review of the security offered in earlier versions of IIS, go to the Delta Guide series Web site at www.deltaguideseries.com and enter article ID# **A020301**.

Locking/Unlocking a Server

The easiest way to keep something secure it is to never grant people access to it unless they absolutely need it. You don't go around giving your front door key to everybody; the same basic rules apply to Windows Server 2003 and its approach to IIS.

There are three main steps between the unavailability of IIS when Windows Server 2003 is first installed to a running, functional, but still secure state:

1. Installing IIS (including upgrading from IIS 4/5)

2. Unlocking Static Content

3. Unlocking Web Services Extensions

We're going to have a look at these steps, with a minor detour as we look at the issues when upgrading from a previous version of IIS, and how they both affect and protect the way in which you share and serve your Web sites.

Installing IIS

This has already been covered in Chapter 1, "Introducing IIS 6," but at the risk of repeating myself, it's worth mentioning that this is absolutely the best and most fundamental way of securing your servers from an attack through the IIS service.

To add IIS to an existing system, you need to use the Configure Your Server Wizard, available through the Administrative Tools folder in your Start menu.

INSTALLING EXTENSIONS
Remember that when you install IIS, you need to confirm whether you want to include FrontPage Extensions or ASP.NET functionality.

If you've already installed IIS (or any of the other roles) and you want to remove the role from your server, using the same wizard, select the role you want to remove (IIS is part of the Application server role), and click Next.

You will be prompted to confirm the removal of IIS and the disabling of the ASP.NET service if you installed it. Note that it won't remove any of your Web sites or documents—just the application and services used to support the service.

The removal of the application is complete and absolute—if you later choose to add IIS to your server again, you will need the CD to install it. The removal really does purge the necessary components from the installation.

Upgrading from IIS 4/5

When you upgrade from Windows 2000 and IIS 5, or from Windows NT and IIS 4, Windows Server 2003 should automatically pick up any of the sites you've configured on these machines and server just as if you'd set them up on a new machine.

However, if you upgrade a machine from either of these two platforms and you have not modified the basic setup of IIS, Windows Server 2003 disables the service. This affords the same level of protection as installing Windows Server 2003—IIS is not installed unless you ask it to be.

Unlocking Static Content

Once IIS has been installed and enabled through the Server Roles Wizard, it's still more secure than a base IIS 4 or 5 installation. In its default state, IIS is only capable of serving static Web pages. All dynamic content, including CGI and ASP based content, is not enabled.

FRONTPAGE EXTENSIONS

If you elected to install FrontPage extensions when you were running the Configure Your Server Wizard, the FrontPage ISAPI filter is already installed and configured on your IIS sites.

Static content is therefore unlocked as soon as you install IIS, but IIS still has some additional tricks to prevent users from downloading files they shouldn't have access to.

 ## WEB RESOURCE

For a tutorial on setting basic directory based authentication, go to the Delta Guide series Web site at www.deltaguideseries.com and enter article ID# **A020302**.

 ## UNLOCK AT YOUR OWN RISK

Don't unlock any IIS functionality that you don't absolutely need. Every piece of functionality—FrontPage Server Extensions, ASP.NET, or whatever—is another "moving part" that hackers can attempt to exploit. Leaving IIS locked down will help make it as secure and safe as possible.

Recognized File Extensions

In addition to only serving static Web content, IIS also extends its restrictions on what it serves from a site. One problem with previous versions is that IIS would blindly supply any file that happened to be in a directory shared through IIS, whether or not the file is officially listed. This made it possible to download applications, scripts, components, password files—you name it—from a directory if a user accidentally or deliberately entered the correct URL.

IIS 6 will only accept requests for files with extensions that it recognizes. The accepted file types that IIS will provide as static content are controlled through the MIME types settings. Note that it doesn't affect dynamic content, which is controlled through two separate mechanisms in the form of the Web service extensions manager and the file verification system.

You can manage the accepted MIME types that IIS will serve in two different places—at a server level and a Web site/directory level. You can see an example of the default settings, configured at the server level, shown in Figure 3.1.

MIME TYPES

The MIME type is sent back to the client when it requests a file, and it's used by the client to determine how the file should be handled. Remember that when adding a MIME type (and therefore an extension) setting, you should configure the right MIME type. Although most browsers have built-in mappings, most use the server derived information if it's supplied.

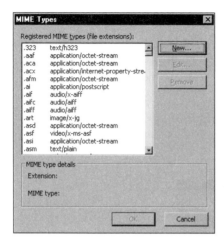

Figure 3.1   Default MIME types configured in IIS.

The Web site/directory level settings augment the settings at the server level; they are not mutually exclusive. For example, if you have enabled Word documents (.doc) at a server level, all Web sites on that server will enable Word documents to be downloaded.

Unfortunately, this means that you have to control the system very carefully. If you have a need to supply specific document types—for example, Word, Excel, Acrobat, and so on—I recommend removing any setting from a server level and instead enabling the settings at the Web site, or better still, directory level.

FOR THE ABSOLUTE BEST IN PROTECTION
I prefer to disable all the file types from the MIME list and then only specifically enable the types that I know I've added to the site or server.

This can also work in your favor if you use the IIS folders to hold additional material about a project or item. For example, you might keep a Word document of a report in the same directory as the HTML version that you are serving. With the default settings, the Word document would be downloadable; with only the HTML files enabled, you can keep the files in the same folder.

Protected Web Content
Most malicious attempts to access and use your IIS server rely on the ability to write files and to update and overwrite configuration files and others through the IIS service.

Within IIS 6, anonymous Web users are blocked from writing to the server, preventing them from making any changes, no matter what tricks they try.

Unlocking Web Services Extensions

Dynamic Web content is supported through the Web services extensions—a new, separate component of the IIS configuration process. Web services extensions include the ISAPI filters and other dynamic content solutions, including ASP, CGI wrappers, and Server Side Includes.

IIS can allow or deny ISAPI filters to execute, improving your security by reducing the risk from the supported—but otherwise uncontrollable—extensions supported under previous versions. They are managed through the Web Services Extensions Manager portion of the IIS Manager, as seen in Figure 3.2.

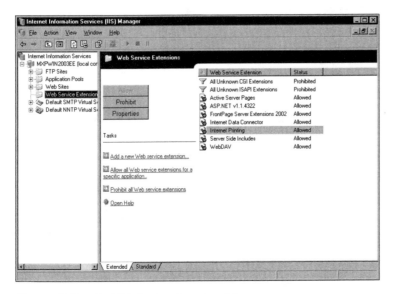

Figure 3.2   The Web Services Extensions Manager.

The two settings for each of the extensions that IIS knows about are as follows:

- **Prohibit**—Prevents the ISAPI DLL from loading (and therefore executing).

- **Allow**—Allows all documents destined for use with the ISAPI filter to be processed.

In either case, the enablement or disablement covers the entire server, so it should be used with caution on multi-host servers.

PROHIBITING EXTENSIONS

You should be careful when prohibiting an extension that is actually in use by a current Web site. Usually IIS can identify the sites that use the extension by looking at the application configurations for different Web sites and directories, but it doesn't always work. Make sure that you know which of your applications (and Web sites) need which extensions.

In general, you should leave all the extensions in their default prohibited state unless you need them. Remember that you still have to enable applications (and if necessary, a corresponding application pool) to actually allow these extensions to be used, but that doesn't mean you can be careless. A list of the default Web Service Extensions and their security settings are given in Table 3.1.

TABLE 3.1 Default Web Service Extension Security Settings

Web Service Extension	Notes
All Unknown ISAPI Extensions	You should leave this set to prohibited. Allowing unknown ISAPI extensions will make your system more susceptible to worm and virus attacks, such as the NIMDA/Code Red.
All Unknown CGI Extensions	You should leave this to prohibited and then only allow CGI extensions that you have specifically allowed.
Active Server Pages	Used to support the old ASP standard.
ASP.NET	Used to support the new ASP.NET standard and pages developed within the .NET Framework.
FrontPage Server Extensions	Used to support FrontPage extensions. You must enable this if you want users to administer and publish Web sites from a client computer, especially through tools such as FrontPage.
Internet Data Connector	Used to support simpler dynamic Web pages that display data from a database. If you are using ASP for your dynamic sites, you can usually leave this as prohibited.
Server Side Includes (SSI)	Used to support the SSI system and best left prohibited unless you specifically need the SSI system. If you are using ASP and SSI together, consider moving your templates entirely to ASP and disabling SSI support.
WebDAV	Used for the Web Distributed Authoring and Versioning System, which can be used to allow authenticated users to publish, lock, and manage files and resources on a Web site. WebDAV is generally more practical than FrontPage, but it's also a more open security risk if not properly managed, so make sure that it's prohibited unless required.

Adding a New Web Service Extension

The Web Service Extension Manager only allows or prohibits the use of the extensions it knows about. If you've got an ISAPI filter that you've added to the system and are merely using it directly from within the application configuration, the extension manager can't control it.

This means that if you want to be able to arbitrarily deny access to a given filter, you should add it to the Web Service Extension Manager.

To do this, right-click on the Web Service Extensions folder and choose Add New Web Service Extension. You will see the window as shown in Figure 3.3. You will need to give the extension a name and then list the DLLs that make up the filter.

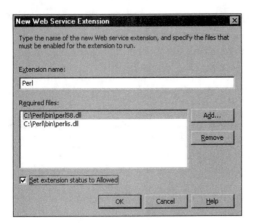

Figure 3.3   Adding a new Web service extension.

Prohibiting All Access

You can switch off all the Web service extensions by right-clicking the Web Service Extensions object within IIS manager and selecting Prohibit All Web Service Extensions.

The obvious time you might find this useful is if you suspect that an attack is currently taking place and you want to disable dynamic content while leaving static content in place. It can also be useful if you are upgrading or updating a site and need to provide a placeholder page to indicate the status while the site is upgraded.

File Verification

Before IIS 6 processes a request for some dynamic content that has to be processed by an ISAPI filter, it checks that the requested content actually exists. This prevents users from using exploits that execute or trigger a response in an ISAPID filter, regardless of the actual document they are asking for.

With this system in place, it should be impossible to make use of an exploit in an ISAPI— even one that has somehow been installed maliciously—unless the filter itself is compatible with, and able to access, a file in the first place.

Authentication Methods

In IIS 4 and 5, a number of authentication solutions were available. The primary methods were those that integrated into the local- or domain-based user/password systems.

Although time has moved on, there aren't many new mechanisms available to us that provide additional authentication solutions. The original built-in systems still exist—anony-mous authentication, basic authentication, integrated windows authentication, and digest authentication. As before, IIS will also authenticate users who it can identify as being within the AD.

Two new authentication systems are available in IIS 6, however—Passport Integration and Constrained/Delegated Authentication. The former is designed as an alternative to the existing mechanisms. The latter is a new way of assigning authentication credentials to an application so that it can communicate with other servers or backend services, such as SQL databases in the process of processing a request.

A third authentication system is available programmatically through the ASP.NET Web service extension. This provides mechanisms to authenticate a user for an application and provides pass through facilities to the Windows and AD authentication systems and the new Passport system.

 WEB RESOURCE

For a tutorial on setting security based on the hosts visiting your sites, go to the Delta Guide series Web site at www.deltaguideseries.com and enter article ID# **A020303**.

Passport Integration

We are generally used to the idea of Single Sign On (SSO) within the office environment— you log in to your Windows machine, and this provides you with access to all the servers, Intranet sites, and email services, for example. But what happens when we extend that to the Internet?

PILES OF PASSWORDS

I know I have a lot of passwords and login information across a range of Web sites—but it would be much more convenient if I could just use the same login and password, in a secure fashion, to gain me access to the sites I use regularly.

This is the point of Passport—a central Web site that holds credential and user information which can then be shared among other participating sites. IIS 6 incorporates the capability to communicate directly with the Passport system and authenticate your users through their Passport identities.

You can enable Passport authentication on Web sites served by your own IIS implementations by selecting the .NET Passport authentication. When a user connects to your Web site, IIS will look for a Passport cookie with the user's Passport identity. If the user has a cookie, he is redirected to the main Passport.net site to have his password verified. Once he has logged in correctly, he will be redirected back to the original URL. If he doesn't have a cookie, he is prompted to create one on the Passport site.

PASSPORT AND OTHER AUTHENTICATION TYPES

Passport cannot be used in conjunction with other authorization types because Passport operates with cookies rather than the standard HTTP-based authorization system. Therefore, you can only configure a site or directory to support Passport or any other authorization system combination, but not both.

If you need to provide specific access to an area of your site through Passport, you can map users within your Active Directory domain to a known Passport user, and then use the standard security controls and access control lists, merely using Passport as a login mechanism.

PASSPORT REQUIRES EFFORT!

Passport isn't something you can casually turn on and start using. You will need to become an official Passport Web Site, which involves paying fees to Microsoft and implementing special software. It can take several weeks or more to get fully integrated with Passport, and fees can run into several thousands of dollars per year.

Constrained, Delegated Authentication

If you are supporting a distributed application or are using remote UNC paths to support a local Web service, it's important to be able to retain security between the machines running these services to prevent malicious use or accidental failures causing serious problems.

Windows Server 2003 introduces a system of constrained, delegated authentication. This enables a user to be given access to specific types of services on specific servers as if he were accessing the system locally. Essentially, the primary server—that is, the IIS service—masquerades as the user.

The two recommendations to the use of constrained, delegated authentication according to Microsoft are as follows:

- Delegation should not enable a server to connect on behalf of the client to *any* resource in the domain/forest. This is the constrained portion of the system; it defines that users (and servers supporting user access) should be granted access only to specific services—for example, to the SQL service on a given server—rather than to a SQL service on any server, or any service on any server.

- Delegation should not require the client to share its credentials with the server. This reduces the chances of malicious attacks by enabling the communication to take place without actually exchanging user and password information, removing the ability to snoop and collect the credentials data.

To configure servers to use the constrained, delegated authentication system, you must configure individual server affiliations through the Active Directory Users and Computers tool by setting server and authentication systems.

You can get more information on the steps required to enable authentication at the Microsoft Windows Server 2003 Deployment guide; the URL for the relevant page is `http://www.microsoft.com/technet/treeview/default.asp?url=/technet/prodtechnol/windowsserver2003/deploy/confeat/remstorg.asp`.

ASP.NET Based Authentication

For authentication within an application, IIS 6 and ASP.NET provide three main forms of authentication system supported by a number of authentication providers within the ASP.NET system:

- **Windows authentication**—This uses the authentication provided by the standard IIS 6 authentication mechanisms and interface (that is, digest, integrated, and so on).

- **Passport authentication**—Works just like the integrated IIS-based Passport authentication system, but because it can be built into an ASP application, you can provide a friendlier interface.

- **Forms-based authentication**—Enables a developer to use a standard ASP form to request credentials that can then be authenticated through the standard mechanisms or a built-in solution.

ASP.NET applications can directly make use of this authentication, and in turn the information can be used with the authorization system.

Authorization

IIS 6 incorporates a new authorization framework designed to extend the object-based authorization system in previous versions. The object-based system restricted access based on the access control list for file or directory, which was based on the settings applied to the underlying storage mechanism (typically an NTFS file system).

However, it's impossible to use this with a dynamic-based Web application because the application could provide a number of different facilities through the same file. These applications are task based, and restricting access on this basis required that the developer build his own system that could control access based on his authentication credentials and a built-in authorization role.

The new authorization framework allows developers to add and extend the authorization system to provide mechanisms that can work with the existing authentication system from within their application to authorize different areas of their system based on roles, tasks, and other criteria.

The main solution at the time of release is a URL-based authorization system that can apply authorization policy within a given application and therefore against specific URLs rather than objects. The authorization policies can be stored independently of the application and then shared among a number of applications.

The system relies on the .NET Framework and can also be used and applied within ASP.NET applications directly. Configuring the system is beyond the scope of this book, so check the Windows documentation for more information.

SSL Improvements

The Secure Sockets Layer in IIS 5 was already quite a capable system but contained a few minor annoyances that could be difficult to get around. IIS 6 has made a number of minor and some more significant improvements. The main features are

- **Performance** has been increased by as much as 50% on an implementation that was already one of the fastest in the business.

- **Selectable Crypto-service providers** allow you to use third-party hardware-based accelerator cards for encrypting information over SSL. Because SSL is a significant CPU performance hog, this can improve the speed of SSL-heavy Web sites.

- **Remote Administration** of certificates is now supported by enabling remote support in the cryptographic API (CAPI) certificate store. When managing many hundreds or thousands of sites, this eases administration considerably.

IIS 6 also incorporates two new wizards to help in configuring and managing the certificates: the Web Server Certificate Wizard and the Certificate Trust List Wizard.

Web Server Certificate Wizard

The Web Server Certificate Wizard is used to obtain, configure, and renew server certificates. The wizard is capable of creating a certificate request, replacing a server certificate (from an online or offline certificate service or from a file), reassign a certificate from one Web site to another, or simply view certificate information. It can also identify existing certificates and their expiry.

When creating a new certificate, you can select both the security level and the cryptographic service provider. To request a new server certificate using the Web Server Certificate Wizard, follow these steps:

1. In IIS Manager, expand the local computer, and then expand the Web Sites folder.

2. Right-click the Web site or file that you want, and then click Properties.

3. On the Directory Security or File Security tab, under Secure communications, click Server Certificate.

4. In the IIS Certificate Wizard (Figure 3.4), click Create a New Certificate.

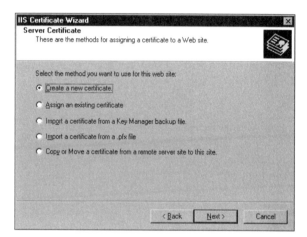

Figure 3.4 Creating a new certificate with the IIS Certificate Wizard.

5. Choose whether you want to prepare the request for sending or whether you want to send it immediately. We'll follow the preparation process; the core certificate requirements are, of course, part of both systems. Click Next.

6. You will be asked some basic information about the certificate (Figure 3.5). Enter the name of the Web site (this is, its friendly, identifiable name, rather than its domain name) and the required bit length for the key (the longer, the more secure), and choose whether you want to select the cryptographic service provider. If you select this last option you will go through an interim screen before the next step, asking you to choose the service provider. Click Next.

7. Fill in the organization information—that is, the legal organization name and the organizational unit (division or department). Click Next.

8. Enter the common name of your site. If it's a public site, enter the fully qualified domain name of the machine, or the domain it's in. If it's an intranet site, use the machine's basic name or NetBIOS name. Click Next.

9. Enter the country, state, and city in which you are located. Click Next.

10. Enter the filename where the certificate request can be stored. Click Next.

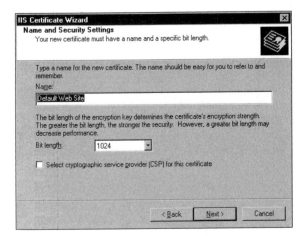

Figure 3.5 Entering basic site information when creating a certificate request.

> 11. You will see a summary of all the options, similar to the one seen in Figure 3.6. Click Next to accept the settings and create the request.

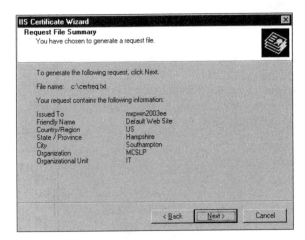

Figure 3.6 Summary information for a new secure certificate.

> 12. Click Finish.

You will need to mail the certificate request to a suitable authority who will then send you the real certificate.

As with any wizard, the steps are relatively easy to follow, and it should be easy enough to follow the steps for all the different tasks supported by the wizard.

Certificate Trust List Wizard

The Certificate Trust List Wizard enables you to configure trust relationships between servers and certification authorities so that you can control which certification authority certificates from a client can be trusted on your site. You do this by creating a certificate trust list (CTL) that, in turn, is handled by the wizard.

Microsoft recommends the following guidelines when assigning IP addresses, Web sites, and SSL ports to your server certificates:

- You cannot assign multiple server certificates per Web site.

- You can assign a certificate to multiple Web sites.

- You can assign multiple IP addresses per Web site.

- You can assign multiple SSL ports per Web site.

You can follow the steps in the Certificate Trust List Wizard to create and edit CTLs. You can get to the CTL Wizard by going to the Security tab for a Web site, directory, or file and clicking on the Edit button within the Secure Communications panel. Click on the check box in the properties window (see Figure 3.7). Choose an existing CTL or access the wizard to edit the currently selected CTL by clicking Edit. You can also create a new CTL through the wizard by clicking New.

Figure 3.7   Setting secure communication options.

Worker Process Identification

Security isn't only about authentication and authorization; it's also about the stability of your server because, in general, some form of instability tends to suggest a potential weak point in the server.

The new execution structure of IIS is whether Worker Process Isolation mode or IIS 5 Compatibility create a secure environment because the individual processes that actually service the Web applications can be so finely controlled, including enabling them to be recycled manually or automatically.

In both isolation modes, we can also secure individual application pools by assigning them a specific user account under which to execute. IIS 6 has updated and extended the available options, so it's worth covering the entire range now available:

- **ASPNET**—A local user account specifically designed to be used with the ASP.NET worker process (`aspnet_wp.exe`) application only when the server is running in IIS 5 isolation mode.

- **Local System**—Default user configured for all IIS and Indexing Service users. Worker processes configured with this user have access to the entire system (and should therefore be avoided).

- **Local Service**—A limited privilege account granting access to the local system only. You should use this only when applications do not need access to other servers within a networked application.

- **Network Service**—Provides a higher level service than that provided by the Local Service, including the ability to log on as a server and to communicate with other servers. This is the default account for worker processes in worker process isolation mode.

- **IUSR_ComputerName**—The guest account used by anonymous users accessing an Internet Web site. If disabled, anonymous access to the site is disabled.

- **IWAM_ComputerName**—The guest account used with Web applications. If disabled, this account blocks out of process applications when operating in IIS 5 Isolation mode.

The IIS_WPG group is granted the minimum rights required to start a worker process.

Table 3.2 summarizes the main rights for each user.

TABLE 3.2 Default User Rights for Special IIS Users

User Right	ASPNET	Local Service	Network System	IUSR	IWAM	IIS_WPG
Access computer from the network	X	X	X	X	X	X
Adjust memory quota for a process		X	X		X	
Allow log on locally				X		
Bypass traverse checking		X	X	X	X	
Generate Security Audit		X	X			
Impersonate a client after authentication	X					X
Log on as a batch job	X	X		X	X	X
Log on as a service	X		X			
Deny Log on through terminal services	X					
Replace a process-level token		X	X		X	
Deny log on locally	X					

CGI APPLICATIONS
If you create a new user to be used with application pools for the purposes of running CGI applications, the user must have been granted the Replace a Process Level Token and Adjust Memory Quotas for a Process rights. You can do this through the Local Security policy manager.

User Management

Users are configured either through the local account mechanism or, if you are within Active Directory, through the AD Users and Groups manager. However, if you want to restrict access, it can be more secure to create local users (which therefore don't automatically have access to AD resources and the rest of the domain) on a local basis.

When you have a new user, you can grant him access to the various facilities within IIS by using the Local Security Policy Manager to set specific rights. Just go to Local Policies, User Rights Assignment.

If you are using domain accounts, use the Group Policy editor and create a new policy within Computer Configuration, Security Settings, Local Policies. You can then apply the group policy to your IIS servers OU accordingly.

Setting Identity in Worker Process Isolation Mode

When working in worker process application mode, you can change the identity of an application pool using the following steps:

1. Right click on the application pool.

2. Select Properties from the popup menu.

3. Select the Identity tab (see Figure 3.8).

Figure 3.8 Setting worker process identity.

4. Choose a predefined identity or click the Configurable radio button and enter the username and password for the user you want to use.

5. Click OK

Setting Identity in IIS 5 Isolation Mode

IIS 5 Isolation mode can also set a user to be used for pooled applications using the following steps:

1. Open the Component Services tool from the Administrative Tools folder in the Start menu.

2. Expand the Component Services node, the My Computer node, and the COM+ Applications node.

3. Right-click the IIS Out-of-Process Pooled Applications entry and select Properties.

4. You will be presented with a window similar to the one shown in Figure 3.9. Here you can choose one of the System accounts or a specific user by entering the user's ID and password.

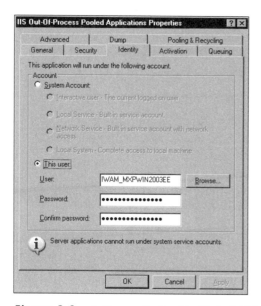

Figure 3.9 Setting application identity in IIS 5 Isolation mode.

5. Click OK.

Background Security

The term background makes it sound as if these are less important, when in fact some are just as, if not more, important than the built-in features offered within specific areas.

Certainly preventing IIS from ever being installed at a domain level through group policy is a good way of completely eliminating IIS as a threat.

Controlling IIS Through Group Policy

Windows Server 2000 included an extensive range of group policies that can be used and applied to the users and computers within domains, and can control everything from basic password and user parameters to the specific configuration of certain elements of the operating system.

Windows Server 2003 has quite considerably increased the number of elements and areas that can be configured through the policy system. You can still configure user account and auditing settings through the group policy system, which you can use to help control the authentication and access to your site.

Also introduced in the new version is the ability to prevent users from installing IIS, or applications that required IIS, on Windows Server 2003 machines. You can use this to control IIS installations at the departmental or location/branch office level. You can also use it to protect other servers within your network on which you don't want IIS enabled—for example, a file or database server.

EXISTING IIS INSTALLATIONS

Unfortunately, the policy doesn't stop or otherwise disable existing IIS installations, only new ones. However, if you set up the policy, apply it to the servers and then remove IIS; it will stop new installations from occurring.

The policy is within Computer Configuration, Administrative Templates, Windows Components, Internet Information Services, Prevent IIS installation. There are only three settings:

- **Enabled**—Installation is prevented.

- **Disabled**—Machines within the domain tree are specifically allowed to install IIS.

- **Not Configured**—The usual propagation rules apply.

Command Line Tool Access

Previous versions of IIS allowed command-line tools to be executed by Web applications. Sometimes this was needed for the sake of convenience; other times, it was a requirement of the application. In IIS 6, it's impossible, even as an Administrator, to execute command-line tools. This not only eliminates the ability to run most of the command line administration tools, but also prevents some viruses and worms from running and propagating.

Timeouts and Limits

Some exploits in IIS have used the long timeouts and often large limits. For example, when running a denial of service attack, the excessively long timeouts make it easy to saturate the server with a relatively small number of clients.

Also, applications served by IIS could cause performance problems and security issues by overflowing the memory and CPU with requests if there were a problem with the application or supporting libraries in some way.

The new worker process model helps alleviate this slightly by building in protection in the form of renewable processes for servicing user requests. But the limits have also been lowered so that IIS is more likely to identify an issue with an application or system before it really does start to cause problems.

Updates and Patches

One reason that the Code Red and NIMDA worms spread quite quickly and voraciously was because of an unknown exploit in IIS. Microsoft was quick to react when the worms started to spread by releasing a patch within a few days that stopped the worms dead in their tracks. In fact, an earlier patch to the operating system had already addressed one of the known exploits.

Unfortunately, not everybody had applied the patch, and even when the new patch had been released, not everybody listened—either because they didn't care, didn't think the patch or the problem applied to them, or just assumed that because they had a firewall, the problem didn't matter. Of course, the worms used an exploit that bypassed firewalls because to the firewalls it looked like standard traffic.

The bottom line is that you should keep up-to-date with the various patches and fixes that Microsoft makes available. Microsoft has made a solemn pledge with the release of Windows Server 2003 to respond to potential security threats and exploits used in the past as quickly as possible.

In addition to the 'hotfixes' released when a problem occurs and the regular service packs, just as with Windows 2000, Microsoft will also be pumping out regular updates and fixes using the Windows Update Service—the automatic system built in Windows XP and made available through Windows 2000 with Service Pack 3.

You can configure the automatic updates through the System control panel. At an individual server level, you can control how and when these updates are applied by setting the various preferences here. You can see an example of the configuration in Figure 3.10.

If you are running an array of servers and want to control the patches and updates applied to them all without doing so individually, use the Software Update Server (SUS), which provides a local copy of the Windows update service and patches. The settings for the different systems can be applied through group policies so that you can automatically install patches on some servers, whereas others require your intervention.

SUS also caches the information, so you won't download the update multiple times and you get the opportunity to individually approve patches before they get published to the clients.

WIDER SUS USE

SUS downloads all the updates for your chosen platforms that you can use to keep all your workstations and servers up-to-date. Caching the updates, even in a relatively small office, can prevent you from wasting your bandwidth.

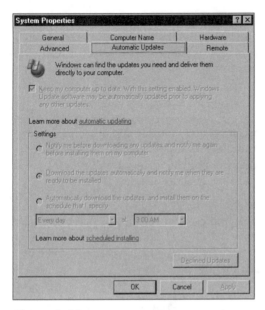

Figure 3.10   Setting update intervals and automatic installation preferences.

FTP Security

Although not used by everybody, FTP is still a common method of providing an alternative way of downloading material from a Web site. Among the obvious benefits of FTP is its easy directory/file listing abilities and the easy method with which clients can upload files and information if they need to.

WebDAV has replaced FTP for most file sharing/uploading requirements, especially for updating and managing Web site information.

An alternative, and sometimes more common, use for FTP was for the so-called 'dropbox' used to communicate between clients. The idea of the dropbox is to provide an outgoing directory from internal users to supply files to a client, and incoming users to have an incoming box into which they could drop files. From the client's perspective, the outgoing box could be read and viewed, but not written to, whereas the incoming box could be written to, but the contents not viewed.

With previous versions of IIS, however, FTP was less than ideal for both Web site updating and dropbox needs. All FTP users were placed into the same global directory when they logged in, making it possible for clients to view or at least identify the Web sites and directories of other clients.

IIS 6, on the other hand, includes the capability to isolate users from each other—when an authorized user logs in, he can be placed in his own directory that is separate and secure from other users and the anonymous user directory. Three modes are available—Non-isolated mode, Isolated Mode, and Isolated Mode using Active Directory.

You cannot switch between the different modes at will; instead, you must select the corresponding mode according to your requirements when you create a new FTP site. If you want to change the mode of an existing FTP site, you will need to re-create it.

 FTP OVER SSL

FTP can be made more secure by running over Secure Sockets Layer (SSL), but unfortunately IIS doesn't include an SSL variation. If you're interested in using FTP over SSL, you will need to look elsewhere for a solution.

Setting FTP Isolation Modes

You configure the Isolation mode for an FTP site when you are creating the site through the FTP Site Creation Wizard. To create a new FTP site and select the FTP User Isolation mode, follow these steps:

1. In IIS Manager, expand the local computer (or a remote one).

2. Select the FTP Sites folder; then right-click, choose New and then FTP Site.

3. Give the new site a identifying description. Click Next.

4. Choose an IP address and port number. Click Next.

5. Choose the FTP user Isolation mode. Click Next.

6. If you are creating a non-isolated or isolated FTP site, enter or use Browse to select the location of your FTP root directory. Click Next.

7. If you are creating an FTP site using the isolated using Active Directory mode, enter the username and password to be used to gain access to the specified active directory domain. Click Next.

8. Select the permissions (read and/or write) for the FTP site. Click Next.

INSTALLING FTP SERVICES

The FTP service is not installed by default when you install IIS using the Configure Your Server Wizard. To add FTP (and other) services to your IIS installation, you will need to use the Add/Remove Programs tool (in Control Panels). Switch to the Add/Remove Windows Components manager and drill down through the Application Server and IIS details until you can select the FTP service. You will probably need the Windows Server 2003 CD to finish the installation.

Depending on which isolation mode you have chosen, there might be some additional steps. These are included in the following sections, along with information on the performance and security affects each mode has.

Non-Isolated Mode

In Non-isolated mode, IIS 6 works in the same fashion as IIS 4/5—users connecting to the site, anonymous or authorized, are placed in the same home directory as configured for the FTP site.

Isolated Mode

In Isolated mode, you can continue to have both anonymous and authorized users. However, anonymous and authorized users are placed in different directories.

If you are supporting anonymous connections, configure the user who needs to be used when granting access rights (see Figure 3.11); then create a directory called LocalUser within the configured FTP root directory for this site and create another directory within LocalUser called Public. Anonymous users will be placed into this directory when they log in.

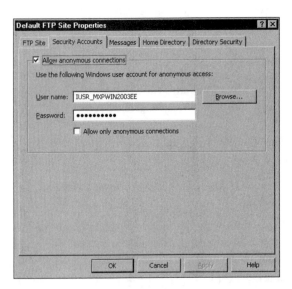

Figure 3.11 Granting access rights for FTP users.

For each authorized user, create a corresponding directory within the LocalUser directory. For example, the user MBrown would have a directory called LocalUser\MBrown. If your users will also specify their domain during log in, create an intermediary domain directory in place of LocalUser. That is, Sales\MBrown would be located within Sales\MBrown.

The main issue with isolated mode is that the initial login can be quite slow because it has to check the name across the entire domain and then locate the corresponding directory within the tree. It also restricts user directories to a location within the main FTP root, which isn't always practical.

On the plus side, the administration is much easier if you are creating a system for hundreds of users because you don't need to manually edit each user's properties.

Isolated Mode Using Active Directory

The Active Directory method is probably the easiest and most straightforward to work with for a small numbers of users because it enables you to control the user directories through the user's properties. It can also be faster because it verifies the credentials against a specific part of the active directory.

If you choose this method of isolation, IIS makes use of two new properties that have been added to the Active Directory schema for a user object. The FTPRoot property relates to the Universal Naming Convention (UNC) of the file server share on which the directory is located and FTPDir is the subdirectory within that share for the user. The combination of the two will be used as the user's home directory when he logs in via FTP.

FILE SHARING AND FTP

Because this mode uses the file sharing system to provide the user's home directory, the server used for the system must have file sharing enabled.

As with the standard isolated mode, anonymous users are supported and the root directory set within the properties for the FTP site used as the directory for these users. However, the username applied to anonymous connections should be a user within the Active Directory domain rather than a local user.

Setting PASV Port Ranges

Passive FTP mode uses a different port number for sending files back to the client than the default FTP port of 21, which is used to send commands and responses.

You can't configure IIS to switch off passive FTP port support, but in IIS 6 you can configure the port range used, which makes it easier to select a port range and configure your firewall service to pass through the passive FTP traffic.

There is no front end for the configuration, but it can be set by directly modifying the XML metabase for IIS. The PassivePortRange property within the /LM/MSFTPSVC path should be used to specify the range of ports for PASV support.

For more information on editing the IIS Metabase, see the next chapter.

Management and Monitoring

What's New

When IIS was originally introduced, Web sites were fairly insignificant. Although Microsoft and others expected you to use IIS for Web serving, the reality was that it wasn't seen as the primary purpose of the underlying OS or IIS as a whole.

Obviously things changed fairly rapidly—between the release of Windows 2000 Server products and Windows Server 2003, the number, range, and pervasiveness of Web sites is significant. It's getting difficult to find companies that aren't represented on the Internet, rather than the other way around.

But if we have more Web sites, we need some way of managing them. IIS Manager (formerly Internet Services Manager) remains the primary interface to managing sites, but IIS Manager is not always available, accessible, or useful.

There are four major changes in the area of Web site administration—the use of an XML Metabase the most significant. The remaining three changes are the new Web-based administration system, the extension of the Windows Management Instrumentation (WMI), and a more extensive suite of command-line tools.

Previous versions of IIS have used a binary configuration file—the Metabase—to store all their information. This could be easily backed up and copied to other machines but not edited. IIS 6 allows you to edit the configuration of

IIS by modifying the appropriate XML, even while IIS is actually running. In fact, some features can only be enabled by modifying the Metabase directly.

The other management enhancements are also designed to make it easier to manage the system both remotely and when the system is part of a larger array of Windows Server 2003 computers serving a range of sites. We'll be looking at these additional administration systems in this chapter, starting with the XML Metabase.

Some changes might not be seen as improvements, though. On the management side, one of the most fundamental changes is the removal of the Web administrators group—you must now be a full administrator (or a member of the administrators group) to control IIS. The reason for this is that IIS 6 is seen as an application server with the potential, through malicious or careless use, to open up your machine to attack.

The last section in this chapter looks at the improvements to the logging system. Logs can provide a surprisingly useful range of information for more than just marketing to produce visitor counts. They can, however, be relatively resource hungry because it takes a small amount of time to collate and write the log information, not to mention the fact that the logs can physically take up a lot of storage space. IIS 6 makes a number of improvements here through some extensions to the core logging types and a brand new binary log format.

XML Metabase

All applications have to store their configuration information somewhere. Traditionally, under Windows, this has been the registry. In the case of IIS, configuration data was instead stored in a binary file called the Metabase. This file could be independently backed up, copied, and modified with the appropriate (and hard to find) tools.

IIS 6 still uses a Metabase, but instead of the hard to use and edit binary format configuration file, a text-based, XML formatted Metabase is used. This provides a number of advantages, which nearly all boil down to the same basic fact—as an XML file, we can edit and extract the elements we want in more than just the IIS manager, even using Notepad.

XML

If you are not familiar with XML, it's probably best described as HTML, but without the strict rule set on which tag names we can use. For example, in HTML we know that `<TITLE>` is used to define the page title of a document, but it's only through the definition of the HTML standard that we know this is the case. XML on the other hand is freeform. It's still text based, making XML accessible through a standard text editor. In XML, you can create your own tags, making XML a structured, text-based, storage mechanism. There's a pretty good introduction in the Metabase section of the online help—look for "Metabase Configuration File."

The same basic feature also means that we can copy configuration information between machines, making it ideal in a multi-machine configuration for sharing site parameters or for setting up Web load balancing clusters where the same parameters must be applied to all the servers supporting the sites we are balancing.

 XML IS BETTER

IIS' new XML-based Metabase plays a significant role in its capability to scale out. Much of Microsoft Application Center 2000 was geared toward replicating IIS' configuration; with the new Metabase and with NLB built into all editions of Windows Server 2003, a major piece of Application Center 2000 is now built into the OS.

In this section, we're going to look at setting and editing parameters in the file and at how we can share information and configuration settings by extracting information from an XML Metabase and copying it elsewhere.

Structure of the Metabase

The Metabase schema (stored in MBSchema.xml) file contains a description of the expected layout, components, and properties of the main Metabase file. The Metabase itself is stored in the Metabase.xml file. Both of these files can be found in %systemroot%\System32\Inetsrv.

EDITING THE METABASE SCHEMA
Although the Metabase schema is theoretically editable, you should only do it through the ADSI or Admin Base Objects interfaces using a C++ or C# application.

A copy of the Metabase is also kept in memory. The in-memory version of the Metabase is loaded by an IIS component called the Metabase Storage Layer, converting it to an internal, binary format. The Metabase is then copied into the IIS file cache for speedy access. When you use IIS manager to change the configuration, the internal configuration is changed first so that the rest of the IIS system has access to the changes. Periodically, the in-memory copy is then written to disk. If you've enabled the edit while running feature (covered in more depth later in this chapter), this period is 60 seconds—to keep the in-memory copy in sync with the disk version.

In fact, with the edit while running feature enabled, the version in memory is merged with the version on the disk, and the system constantly checks the disk version of the Metabase file to ensure that it's in sync with the in-memory copy.

Within the Metabase file itself, the structure is tree based (as you'd expect from XML), much like the Windows registry. Locations within the Metabase are specified like a directory (using forward slashes), so the root of individual Web sites configured on a server is located within /LM/W3SVC.

The Metabase root where all useful configuration information starts is actually /LM (short for local machine); within this are the main roots of the top-level configuration for IIS, such as configured extensions, Logging settings, the MIME map, and the root of the individual Web services.

Some examples of additional locations within the Metabase are listed in Table 4.1.

TABLE 4.1   Some Key Locations Within the Metabase File

Location	Description
/LM/Logging	Logging configuration.
/LM/MimeMap	Contains details of all the MIME maps that apply to all Web sites.
/LM/MSFTPSVC	Location of the settings for the FTP service.
/LM/NNTPSVC	Location of the settings for the NNTP service.
/LM/SmtpSvc	Location of the settings for the SMTP service.
/LM/W3SVC	Location of all Web sites configured on the server.
/LM/W3SVC/1	The settings for the first (Default) Web site. Note that the Web site identifier is used, not the Web site name.
/LM/W3SVC/AppPools	Contains details on individual application pools configured within the site.
/LM/W3SVC/Filters	Active ISAPI filters and their settings.
/LM/W3SVC/Info	Settings global to all Web sites.

If you want to change a value in the Metabase, you will be given a location where you can find the property. There are a variety of ways in which you can edit the Metabase, which I cover next.

Editing the Metabase

The obvious way to edit the Metabase is through IIS manager, but we already know that provides a somewhat limited range compared to the full set of available options.

Three primary ways exist in which we can edit the Metabase and set configuration parameters—direct editing, live editing, and Metabase Explorer. Direct editing requires the use of a simple text editor—notepad will do—or you can use a dedicated XML editor. Live editing also uses a text or XML editor, with a slight twist—we can edit the contents of the Metabase while IIS is still running. Metabase Explorer, part of the IIS 6 Resource Kit, provides a more useful and friendly environment.

Direct Editing

Without making any changes from an initial installation, the only way to edit the Metabase outside of IIS Manager is to stop IIS, edit the file using a text editor, and start IIS again. You can see an example of a Metabase file, here open in Notepad, in Figure 4.1.

```
MBSchema.xml - Notepad                                    _ □ ×
File  Edit  Format  View  Help
      <Property    InternalName ="AllowControlMsgs"
      <Property    InternalName ="AllowFeedPosts"               ID="4506
      <Property    InternalName ="AllowKeepAlive"               ID="6038
      <Property    InternalName ="AllowPathInfoForScriptMappings"
      <Property    InternalName ="AlwaysUseSSl"                 ID="3692
      <Property    InternalName ="AnonymousOnly"                ID="5006
      <Property    InternalName ="AnonymousPasswordSync"
      <Property    InternalName ="AnonymousUserName"
      <Property    InternalName ="AnonymousUserPass"
      <Property    InternalName ="AppAllowClientDebug"
      <Property    InternalName ="AppAllowDebugging"
      <Property    InternalName ="AppFriendlyName"              ID="2102
      <Property    InternalName ="AppIsolated"                  ID="2104
      <Property    InternalName ="AppOopRecoverLimit"
      <Property    InternalName ="AppPackageID"                 ID="2106
      <Property    InternalName ="AppPackageName"               ID="2107
      <Property    InternalName ="AppPoolId"                    ID="9101
      <Property    InternalName ="AppPoolIdentityType"
      <Property    InternalName ="AppPoolCommand"               ID="9026
      <Property    InternalName ="AppPoolState"                 ID="9027
      <Property    InternalName ="AppPoolAutoStart"
      <Property    InternalName ="AppRoot"            ID="2103"
      <Property    InternalName ="AppWamClsid"                  ID="2105
      <Property    InternalName ="ArticleTableFile"
      <Property    InternalName ="AspAllowOutOfProcComponents"
      <Property    InternalName ="AspAllowSessionState"
      <Property    InternalName ="AspBufferingOn"               ID="7000
      <Property    InternalName ="AspCodepage"                  ID="7016
      <Property    InternalName ="AspDiskTemplateCacheDirectory"
      <Property    InternalName ="AspEnableApplicationRestart"
      <Property    InternalName ="AspEnableAspHtmlFallback"
      <Property    InternalName ="AspEnableChunkedEncoding"
      <Property    InternalName ="AspEnableParentPaths"
      <Property    InternalName ="AspEnableTypelibCache"
      <Property    InternalName ="AspErrorsToNTLog"
      <Property    InternalName ="AspExceptionCatchEnable"
      <Property    InternalName ="AspKeepSessionIDSecure"
      <Property    InternalName ="AspLCID"           ID="7042"
```

FIGURE 4.1   Editing the Metabase in Notepad.

The only problem with direct editing is that it requires the entire IIS process to be brought down before the file can be edited and written. This means that all your sites and SMTP and FTP services will be down while you edit and update the configuration.

Live Editing

Live Editing gets rid of this limitation. Instead of waiting until the IIS service is shut down, you can just edit the XML Metabase directly— when you save it changes in the file will be reflected almost instantly in the internal memory-located Metabase, and, if the changes are to elements configurable through IIS Manager, immediately viewable and editable in IIS Manager, too.

To enable live editing—also known as the edit while running system—go into IIS Manager, right-click on the machine you want to configure and select Properties (see Figure 4.2). Then check the Enable Direct Metabase Edit check box. Click OK to accept the changes or click Apply to apply them immediately without closing the Properties box.

Once enabled, you can open the Metabase file in any editor and make changes. The result will be the same as opening it before you enabled the edit while running feature. But each time you save the Metabase, it will be merged with the in-memory version.

LIVE EDITING

Take advantage of live editing to reconfigure IIS without taking Web sites offline. You will be a more effective IIS administrator, and you won't inconvenience your site's users!

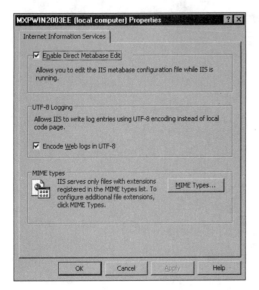

FIGURE 4.2   Enabling Direct Metabase Edit.

Metabase Explorer

Unless you are an XML junkie, editing the Metabase by hand in a text editor, such as Notepad or WordPad, is not going to be much fun. It's much better to use a dedicated tool for editing the information in the Metabase. Although you can find hundreds of different XML editors, none of them currently specialize in editing the IIS Metabase. However, the IIS Resource Kit (available from www.Microsoft.com/downloads) comes with a tool called the Metabase Explorer.

Not exactly a text editor, it does provide a nice easy way to edit and configure all the various options within the Metabase without having to manually trawl through the XML file. You can see an example of Metabase Explorer in action in Figure 4.3.

To edit a property, navigate to the appropriate area—the standard Windows directory/registry tree structure on the left navigates through the major sections, with the properties within the current level shown on the right. To edit a value, just double-click on it.

Occasionally, you need to create new values—the Metabase is not actually pre-populated with all the configurable values. If it were, the file would be huge; one thing of paramount importance in IIS 6 is performance.

To create a property, navigate to the right level, select Edit, and then New. You then need to select whether it's a new key—that is, a navigable folder within the Metabase—or a particular type of property. You need to select the property data type; you will be told which type you need if you need to create a property. For reference, the types are

- String record

- DWORD record

- Binary record

- Multistring record

- Expandable string record

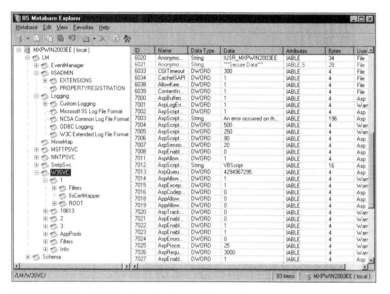

FIGURE 4.3   Editing the Metabase with Metabase Explorer.

LIVE EDITING

I don't, as a rule, recommend editing the Metabase with anything other than Metabase Explorer, even if you are an XML wizard. The plain reason for this is that it is so easy to edit the wrong item, change the wrong property, or accidentally add something in the wrong place.

Corrupt the metabase file during an edit like this, and at best you might just affect a minor part of your Web site configuration. At absolute worst, you could take your entire IIS installation down as you worry about restoring the backup copy.

Backup and Recovery

You can back up the Metabase simply by copying the Metabase and schema files to another location. If you want to incorporate the files into your backup routine, just include the

%systemroot%\System32\Inetsrv directory, which will also back up a number of other useful files.

Backup copies of the Metabase and schema files are also created automatically by default when the configuration changes.

History and Versioning

IIS incorporates an automatic versioning system that provides you with a history of all the changes you have made to the Metabase. These files are created in the history folder, by default located within the %systemroot%\System32\Inetsrv\History folder. The directory stores pairs of files—a copy of each of the schema and Metabase, even if only one of the files has changed. A change is identified as a modification to the in-memory copy of the Metabase; if it identifies a difference when flushing this to disk, the files are copied to the history directory and the new versions are written out.

Naming and Version Numbers

In addition to creating the history files, IIS uses a special system to identify each version. All copies of the Metabase have the name Metabase_majorversion_minorversion.xml, with the schema using the name format MBScheme_majorversion_minorversion.xml.

The majorversion number is incremented by one when

- IIS is manually restarted using the IIS Manager

- IIS is stopped using IIS Manager or the net stop iisadmin command

- During a manual save of the IIS Configuration

- During a normal flush of the in-memory database when changes have been made

---

MANUALLY SAVING THE CONFIGURATION
You can manually save a copy of the configuration by selecting the machine within IIS Manager, right-clicking and selecting All Tasks and then Save Configuration to Disk. A file will only be created if changes have been made to the configuration.

The minorversion number is incremented by one when

- The Metabase is edited while the system is running the edit while in running mode; a version of the Metabase is saved to disk

The minorversion number is always reset when a new major version is incremented.

You can see an example of the history files in Figure 4.4.

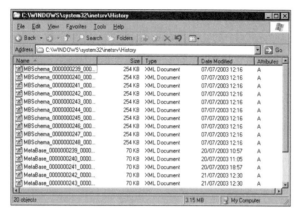

FIGURE 4.4 Automatically created Metabase history files in situ.

History Configuration

Two Metabase properties configure the history file settings. The /LM/EnableHistory settings enables and disables the creation of history files. By default, this setting is set to true (one) so that history files are created. If you want to disable the creation of history files—which I don't recommend—you will need to create this setting and then set the value of the property to 0.

Remember that if you disable the history system, you will lose the automatic backup system. If you have no other backup mechanisms, there might be no other way of recovering from a fault.

You can also configure the number of history files that are kept. By default, only the last 10 copies of the history files are kept—the oldest one is removed each time, so it's always the most recent 10 files.

You can increase or decrease the number of files by editing the /LM/MaxHistoryFiles property. Remember that for even a relatively bare configuration with only a few sites in it, each Metabase file and schema pair will take up about 300KB. With a hundred or so sites, you could easily be looking at 1MB each time. Obviously in these days of multi-gigabyte hard disks, this seems like a fairly low risk situation, but keep it in mind.

Error Files

If you make a change to the Metabase that results in a corrupted file, incorrect Metabase structure, or a truncated entry, you will get a file within the history folder of the form MetabaseError_versionnumber.xml.

Importing/Exporting the Metabase

The command-line script `iiscnfg.vbs` is a general-purpose script that allows you to save, copy, import, and export information from the Metabase.

Saving Configurations

At its simplest level, the `/save` command-line option will save a copy of the in-memory Metabase to disk, providing that the configuration has changed.

You can also execute the command from a remote machine using the `/s` command-line switch—for example, to save the configuration of the machine with the IP address `192.168.1.130`

```
iiscnfg /save /s 192.168.1.130
```

It will use your existing credentials to authorize the save, or you can supply your own using the `/u` and `/p` for user and password information. For example, if we needed to supply the administrator information

```
iiscnfg /save /s 192.168.1.130 /u CORP\Administrator /p Password
```

The more useful components of this script are with the export and import tool.

Exporting Configurations

You can directly export configuration information from the Metabase using the `iiscnfg` script, but you have to specify which part of the Metabase you want to export. For example, if you want to export the individual Web site configurations, you would use

```
iiscnfg /export /f export.xml /sp /lm/w3svc /inherited /children
```

A few extras need to be mentioned:

- **/f**—Specifies the name of the file to which the information will be exported.

- **/sp**—Specifies the topmost node from the metabase to be exported. In this case, we're exporting everything below /LM/W3SVC.

- **/inherited**—Tells the script to export everything from the file under that node, including specific elements inherited from further up the file.

- **/children**—Specifies that all children of this node should be exported to the file.

Importing Configurations

You can also import the information back again. The big benefit here is that you can use it to duplicate Web site definitions, both across the same machine and across different machines.

For example, given the information we've exported previously, we could import that onto another machine to duplicate the site definitions. To do this, we basically run the process in reverse:

```
iiscnfg /import /f export.xml /sp /lm/w3svc /dp /lm/w3svc /inherited /children
```

The /sp specifies where within the source file the script should start importing information, and the /dp specifies where within the current Metabase the information should be imported to. In this case, we've loaded the Web site configuration data into the Web site definition section.

However, a few problems exist that you need to be aware of before blindly copying information between machines in the Metabase file:

- Change or remove references to the current machine within the metabase file because these might affect the machine you are copying the details to.

- Change or create the necessary folders on the destination machine.

- Change any system paths, such as the root folder for IIS Web sites or the folders used to store metabase history files, for example.

- Delete or modify properties relating the IUSR or IWAM accounts, which are unique for each machine.

- Delete any AdminACL properties, which are machine specific and cannot be modified by hand.

- Delete any properties specifying or containing passwords.

If you are copying between machines that will all be part of the same cluster and you are setting them up for the first time, you shouldn't have to worry about the folder or file system paths.

Copying Configurations

Previous versions of IIS provided the IISSync.vbs and IISRepl.vbs scripts, which enabled you to exchange configuration information between servers. We can use the iiscnfg.vbs script to do the same; the only difference is that it's exchanging XML Metabase content.

Unlike the export/import process detailed previously, using the copy command automatically removes all the machine-specific entries that would otherwise cause problems.

If you need to copy information, another alternative is to use the IIS Migration Tool, which is part of the IIS Resource Kit and can migrate IIS 6 sites between machines.

Web-based Management

The idea of a Web interface is not new, having been available in Windows NT and Windows 2000 to a limited extent. As with other areas of IIS, Microsoft has completely rewritten and revamped the Web administration interface.

The main driving force behind this decision was the introduction of the Web Edition of Windows Server 2003. With the probability that a Web Edition server would be without a typical console, there is obviously the need to support alternative methods of managing the server and, in particular, the IIS component.

The reason for this is that the Web Edition is designed to be installed on the rackmount servers now common in data centers and Web farms. Having a display attached to all of these would obviously be difficult to manage. Although there are numerous ways around this, it should be obvious that including display, keyboard, and mouse hardware in each box is an expense in itself, and Keyboard Video Mouse (KVM) switches are not an efficient method of management when you are working with hundreds or even thousands of machines.

Windows Server 2003 addresses this in a number of ways, including extending the support for administration through the command line (which I'll cover later in this chapter in "Command Line Management"), the Remote Desktop Connection (which replaces the old Terminal Services for Administration component and is covered in "Remote Desktop—Terminal Services") and Out of Bandwidth Management (see the following sidebar).

OUT OF BANDWIDTH MANAGEMENT

The problem with many administration solutions, particularly in high-density rackmount installations, is that they rely on network bandwidth and usually a network connection. This isn't a complete solution though; what happens during installation and startup, or during a failure? All these situations cause a problem when networking services are not available and many rackmount devices are 'headless' servers without a console or display adaptor.

Microsoft provides a solution to this problem by supporting the so-called out of bandwidth (OOB) management tools. The Emergency Management Services component can redirect the BIOS and Windows command-line interface to a serial port (or a serial device on a USB adaptor) to allow you to manage and monitor a machine when a network connection isn't available.

Look for "remotely administered servers" and "emergency management services" in the online help for more information on OOB management.

Most of the other tools are generic administration tools first, which then provide IIS management facilities by their design. For example, by supporting desktop access with the Remote

Desktop Connection (RDC) system, you can run IIS Manager as if you were running it locally, as well as providing direct access to the control panels and other admin tools.

The Web interface, however, was designed with the Web Edition specifically in mind and is primarily an IIS configuration tool first—with additional functionality for management of the underlying parts of the OS that help provide or support IIS.

For example, using the Web interface, we can configure Telnet, network interface settings, local users and groups, as well as shut down or restart the server and change the machine's identification—all in addition to setting many of the IIS parameters.

Setting Up Web Management

On Web Edition, the Web-based management system is installed by default. On other editions, you will need to install it by using Add/Remove Server Components applications, drilling down to the World Wide Web Publishing Service (through Application Server, Internet Information Services), and selecting the Remote Administration (HTML) component.

This installs the necessary components and configures a new administration Web site within IIS. The new Web site is configured to work on port 8099 and secure port 8098. However, you must use HTTPS on port 8098 when connecting to the site—if you try to connect without SSL, you will just get a warning page instructing you to try again on the SSL port.

CLIENT SUPPORT

Web Administration requires at least Internet Explorer 5 because it makes use of a combination of HTML standards and some ActiveX controls to support the site functionality. Although other browsers are theoretically supported, in my experience the effects can be less than ideal. Of course, you should have Internet Explorer 6 on your server anyway, and IE 6 is included in Windows XP.

You will also need to supply the credentials to log into the site—obviously an administrative account and password. Once connected and logged in, you will be greeted with a window similar to the one shown in Figure 4.5.

 SECURE THE ADMIN SITE

I recommend configuring the administrative Web site so that only IP addresses used on your internal network can connect. This will help thwart hackers, who consider the administrative Web site a favorite target for attack.

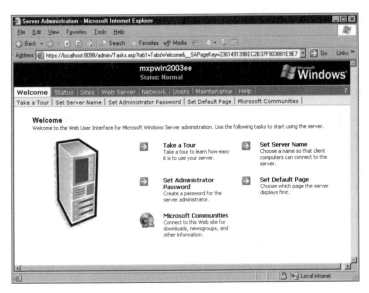

FIGURE 4.5 The initial screen for the Web interface.

The Web Interface

Unsurprisingly, there are a few differences between using the IIS Manager and other tools compared to using the Web interface. The majority of differences all relate to the nature of the Web interface itself. For example, we can't right-click on an object to get its properties, and most of the configuration is handled through a simple Web form rather than a familiar properties window.

It's also worth remembering that the Web interface is an alternative method of configuring the main components of your Web site and server—it's not meant as a replacement for IIS Manager or any of the other tools. If you need a finer level of control and configuration over your servers, you will need to use RDC, IIS Manager on a remote machine connected to the server, or a combination of the command-line tools and manual edits to the Metabase to configure your server.

Beyond these differences and limitations, the Web interface is pretty much what you would expect from an interface constrained by HTML, Web forms, and the largely one-way communication style of HTTP.

You can get a good idea of the basic interface structure by looking back at Figure 4.5. The server name is shown at the top of the window, and any important messages are given under this—initially, you will get one about the SSL certificate being used, which I cover in more detail in "The Status Page."

Beneath the message area, the main blue strip provides the toolbar for the main areas of the site and the white strip beneath that provides the sub-areas. These two button bars provide the main navigation area for the site.

The main portion of the window handles the specific configuration or wizard elements—or on the main heading areas, a summary and description of each of the sub-areas.

Because it's just another method of managing the sites and machine, I only cover the main points and areas of each page and, if necessary, sub-area; the rest should be pretty much self-explanatory.

The Welcome Page

The Welcome page is your first entry point for the administration site, and its prime purpose really is to provide a jump point and basic page for the toolbars. There are a few useful elements here though:

- **Take a Tour**—A quick guide through the various areas of the administration site and the server environment as a whole. Although aimed at people using the administration site on the Web edition, it can be a useful intro to the main components of the site.

- **Set Administrator Password**—Sets a password for the administrator.

- **Microsoft Communities**—Links to the IIS homepage at Microsoft.

- **Set Server Name**—Changes the name of the server and its domain affiliation. This is equivalent to using the Identity tab of the System control panel (see Figure 4.6).

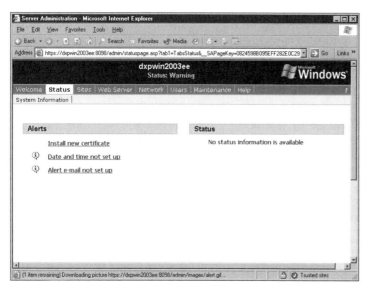

FIGURE 4.6   Setting the Server Name through the Web Interface.

- **Set Default Page**—Allows you to change the default page within the administration site. You can only choose between two—the Welcome page and the Status page, which we'll be looking at next. Unless you have a particular love of the Welcome page, you will probably find the Status page more useful because it will warn you of any significant problems with the server and any sites.

The Status Page

The Status page (see Figure 4.7) is probably the area you will visit the most once your sites are configured and running and everything is, on the whole, working normally.

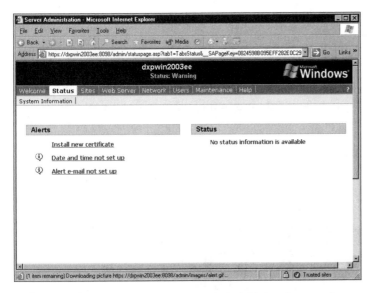

FIGURE 4.7   Monitoring Status through the Web Interface.

It provides a rundown of any major issues or problems with the server. You can get to the page in one of two ways—either directly using one of the toolbars or by clicking on the Status area underneath the server name. The status displayed there will be in one of four colors:

- **Green**—Indicates that everything is running normally.

- **Gray**—Indicates that there is information to pass on that is not important or critical to the operation of your server.

- **Yellow**—Indicates some kind of warning. Either something is not working correctly, hasn't finished being configured, or something that is not yet a problem could be in the future.

- **Red**—Indicates a critical failure or problem somewhere in your Web server or one of your sites.

In each case, if you go to the Status page when the status is in any of the last three states, you will have a list of messages, each a hyperlink, taking you to further information.

INITIAL ERRORS

Depending on what edition you've installed, you will have at least one message in the status error when you first go to the page. In editions other than the Web edition, it will only warn you about requiring a proper SSL certificate for the site. In Web Edition installations, you will have not only that message, but also others warning you to change the administrator password, hostname, and network configuration.

When you click on one of the messages, you will get the full details—shown in Figure 4.8—and you can also optionally clear the message. If you do so, it disappears permanently from the status page, so it's probably best to leave the message until you have actually addressed the issue.

FIGURE 4.8 Getting extended information on errors.

The Sites Page

You can start, stop, and configure the various sites on your machine from the Sites page (see Figure 4.9). As you can see from the figure, you can identify the site by its name, IP address, port number, or its host header. You can also search and find the site you are looking for using any of these criteria.

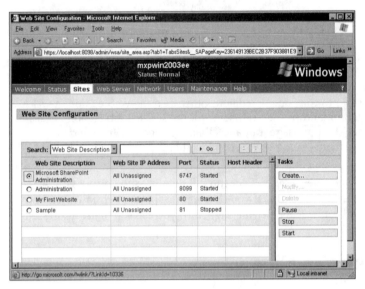

FIGURE 4.9   Site configuration in the Web interface.

You can also modify, pause, start, or stop any of the sites you have configured. The SharePoint admin site (if it's installed) and the default Web site cannot be configured but can be paused, stopped, or started. For obvious reasons, you can't do anything to the administration site.

Also from this window, you can create a new site. The options available to you through this method are not as extensive as those through the wizard and properties pages in IIS manager, but they should be enough to get your site started.

The Web Server Page

The majority of the configuration elements of your server (rather than individual sites) are handled through the Web Server page. Here you can set the 'master' settings, such as the default location for Web sites, script settings, logging preferences, and FTP settings.

These master settings are used as defaults for new sites, and on some pages you get the opportunity to choose whether the changes are made to all sites that use the default settings (including all new sites) or whether they are applied to all sites, irrespective of their current settings. You can see an example of this in the Web Execute Permissions page shown in Figure 4.10.

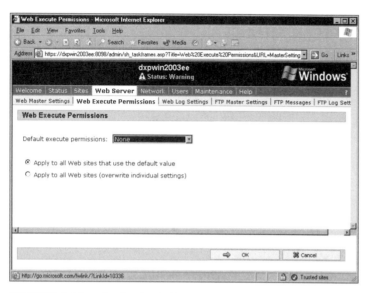

FIGURE 4.10 Configuring Web Execute Permissions.

More specific information for the elements that can be configured through the sub-areas in this section includes

- **Web Master Settings**—Sets the default Web site root directory, ASP timeout, FrontPage Extensions default setting, and the maximum number of connections.

- **Web Log Settings**—Sets the log file format, location, and rotation period as default or all sites.

- **Web Execute Permissions**—Sets the execute permissions for Web sites. One limitation of the Web interface is that script execute permissions can only be configured as either on or off for an entire site—it isn't possible to set them on individual directories. Enabling script access as switched on by default is almost certainly a bad idea.

- **FTP Master Settings**—Sets the default settings, such as enabling content updates through the FTP service, and directory style, as well as general FTP settings, such as timeouts and connection limits.

- **FTP Messages**—Sets the greeting, logout, and maximum connection messages sent to clients.

- **FTP Log Settings**—Sets the log settings for FTP connections and transfers.

USING WEB ADMIN FOR GLOBAL SETTINGS

The Web admin interface can be useful even if you don't necessarily want Web admin facilities because you can set log and other settings right across all the Web sites without any manual configuration. This can make, for example, changing from W3C Extended Log Format to the IIS 6 binary log format across all your sites much easier.

The Network Page

Network settings provide a combination of the facilities available through the Network control panel, the server identification, Administration Web site configuration, and the enabling of the Telnet service. The configuration page for individual interfaces is shown in Figure 4.11.

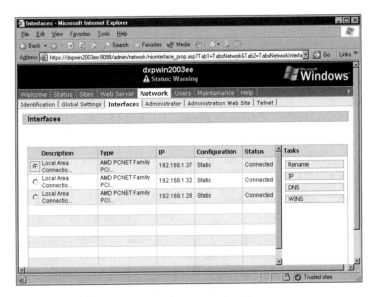

FIGURE 4.11   The Web interface network settings page.

The Network page has the following sub-areas

- **Identification**—Sets the server name and domain membership. This is the true location of the configuration area also available from the Welcome page.

- **Interfaces**—Sets up the parameters for individual network interfaces on the machine. From here, you can set the IP address (including static or DHCP allocation) and the DNS and WINS settings. If you have more than one interface and want to apply the same DNS settings to them all, use the Global Settings page.

- **Administration Web Site**—Configures the port numbers on which the administration site is served and enables you to restrict the IP addresses that can access the site. Note that if you make a change here, although the changes will be submitted, you probably won't get a notification because the server will have changed its port number. You might also need to change the machine from which you are accessing the site. In either case, make sure that you have a record of the changes you've made, so you can access the site again.

- **Global Settings**—Allows you to set global DNS settings across all network interfaces. You can also edit the TCP/IP hosts file and the NetBIOS LMHOSTS file through this area.

- **Administrator**—Changes the Administrator password.

- **Telnet**—Enables or disables access through the Telnet protocol for command-line administration.

LOCKOUT

It's possible, if you are not concentrating, to completely lock yourself out of the system when using some of the pages in this area. In particular, double-check any changes you plan to make to network interface settings, Administrator access, or restricting IP addresses able to connect to the admin site itself.

The Users Page

You can set up the local users and groups through this page. Domain users and groups should be configured on the domain controller or through a server with delegated control.

The Maintenance Page

The Maintenance page is essentially the catch-all page for any elements that didn't really fit into any of the other pages. Personally, I could think of a better place for some of these areas (notably, shouldn't the Logs and Alert E-Mail go under status, and Remote Desktop under Network?), but they are here nonetheless.

The main sections are

- **Date/Time**—Sets the date and time.

- **Logs**—Allows you to view, clear, and download the system logs (Application, Security and System, as through Event Viewer), as well as the Web Administration log. Web logs, curiously, are not directly available online; instead, use Web Server, Web Log Settings to set a log file directory.

- **Alert E-Mail**—Configures the machine to email to any address the messages that apply under any of the three alert stati (critical, warning, and information). If you have a number of servers, this is obviously a more efficient method than continually visiting each admin site.

- **Shutdown**—You can shut down or restart the server from this page. Shutdowns are dangerous unless you happen to be near enough to switch the machine on again. You can also schedule a shutdown or restart for some future time, which can be used to shut down a machine before some scheduled maintenance, for example—useful when many servers are involved and you want to minimize downtime.

- **Remote Desktop**—Allows you to open a connection to the remote desktop connection (RDC) system, which I cover in more detail in "Remote Desktop—Terminal Services."

- **Language**—Changes the language used on the administration site. You can only change this if the main OS has also been configured to work with multiple languages. If only one language is configured for the OS, only one language can be selected within the administration site.

REMOTE DESKTOP
One of the odd things here is that you can't configure whether to enable or disable the remote desktop connection system from within the Web interface—although you can open a connection to it when it's enabled. There doesn't seem to be a good reason for this, and there is no way of enabling it without Administrator access to the system.

Command-line Management

One of the most significant areas generally in Windows Server 2003 has been the improvements and increase in the availability, flexibility, and feature set offered by the command-line utilities.

Windows 2000 Server and Windows NT have always had a reasonable number of command-line tools, and there was talk before Windows 2000 and then again before Windows Server 2003 that the command-line interface would be removed entirely. In the end, the introduction of the Web Edition (which almost requires the command-line interface for some operations) and the extensive use of clients at the long end of a text-only network connection have led Microsoft to not only keep the Command Line Interface (CLI), but also extend it.

Ignoring the specifics of IIS for the moment, Windows Server 2003 incorporates command-line tools that control every aspect of the system.

Even additional features outside the core functionality of the OS are supported by command-line tools, and to an extent IIS is a part of this. The command-line tools in Windows Server 2003 are actually a mixture of direct execution tools and scripts that interface to one of the many interfaces available for administration. We'll have a look at the two main systems, known affectionately as AFSI and WMI, before taking a brief look at the command-line tools available.

The WMI Provider

Web Base Enterprise Management (WBEM) is an industry initiative to standardize the way we access and manipulate information for systems and network devices. WBEM is based on the Common Information Model (CIM)—a system for defining management information that was developed by the Distributed Management Task Force (DMTF).

Microsoft's implementation of the WBEM system is called the Windows Management Instrumentation (WMI). Within Windows Server 2003, the different areas of the OS are those supported by various WMI Providers, including IIS. Scripts, either running VBScript or JScript, can use the WMI Provider to write scripts to perform various tasks—and luckily Microsoft has provided us with a few examples.

Some of these scripts just provide an alternative way to configure or manage the system. Others actually provide a more useful way of displaying or collating information. For example, `iisapp.vbs` allows you to list all the configured applications—something you would otherwise have to trawl through IIS Manager to achieve. You can see a list of the WMI scripts in Table 4.2.

TABLE 4.2 WMI Scripts Provided by Windows Server 2003

Tool	Description
`iisapp.vbs`	Lists the Web applications running on an IIS machine.
`iisback.vbs`	Backs up, restores, lists, and deletes IIS configurations.
`iiscnfg.vbs`	Exports and imports IIS configurations from the Metabase (covered earlier in this chapter).
`iisext.vbs`	Enables and lists applications and Web service extensions and enables you to manage applications and extensions. Provides some of the functionality supported by the Web Services Extensions part of IIS Manager.
`iisftp.vbs`	Allows you to create and manage FTP sites.
`iisftpdr.vbs`	Creates and deletes virtual directories within FTP sites.
`iisvdir.vbs`	Creates and deletes virtual directories within Web sites.
`iisweb.vbs`	Controls Web sites, allowing you to start, stop, create, or delete individual sites.

We unfortunately don't have room to cover all the ins and outs of the scripts; in fact, we've already covered some of the scripts in this and other chapters. If you want more help on these, either supply the `/?` or `/help` command-line option to the command for details on how to use it or check the online help.

The ADSI Provider

Active Directory Services Infrastructure (ADSI) was available in Windows 2000 and provided a Common Object Model (COM) interface to systems configured and managed through the Active Directory as Active Directory Objects. The IIS ADSI provider provides scripted access to IIS properties, such as Web site configurations, directories, and applications.

In IIS 5, ADSI was seen as the way forward for command-line administration, but the WMI system has terminated that particular train of thought. Microsoft hasn't dumped ADSI yet though. ADSI in Windows Server 2003 has been updated to ADSI 2. Unfortunately, this means many of the scripts that work with ADSI won't work with ADSI 2. In particular, the new worker process and IIS 5 isolation modes and application pool systems will play havoc with scripts that update this information.

Enabling Telnet

Telnet provides a command-line interface remotely over a network. Originally a Unix remote login tool, Telnet has now become a recognizable standard for command-line interaction with a number of operating systems.

Windows Server 2003, like Windows 2000, supports Telnet as a network service. By default it's disabled, but it can be started (and set to automatically start) by changing the properties of the service through the Services administration tool.

You can also start and stop the service by using the `tlntadmn` command, although this does not change the default startup mode. The `tlntadmn` command is also the best to set Telnet options, such as the timeout period, the maximum number of connections, and telnet port number.

SECURE ACCESS

Although you still need a valid login and password for Telnet access, the information is still transferred in plain text. If you want a more secure solution, you might want to consider the Secure Shell (SSH) system. This provides a secure, encrypted communication channel using the same basic transport protocol as Telnet, so you can still have command-line access. You can find a Windows version of the SSH server at OpenSSH.org and an SSH and Telnet client called PuTTY at
`http://www.chiark.greenend.org.uk/~sgtatham/putty/`.

For clients, all Windows implementations support a basic telnet client. In earlier implementations this is a separate application, but within Windows XP and Windows Server 2003, it's a command-line level tool that works entirely within the confines of a command prompt.

Recent versions of HyperTerminal also include Telnet support. There's also a wide range of freely available Telnet clients, including my favorite, PuTTY.

Remote Desktop—Terminal Services

Windows 2000 Server products included the Terminal Services system, which was primarily designed to allow remote users to connect to a central server and work, requiring less highly powered desktops and centralizing administration to a smaller number of central servers.

Terminal Services could also be configured to work in remote administration mode so that administrators could remotely connect to and manage a server, just as if they were logged in locally.

The remote administration mode of Terminal Services has been removed. Instead, all Windows Server 2003 computers—whether they have specifically had terminal services enabled or not—support the capability to provide a remote desktop essentially through the terminal services technology. This is based on the same technology that provides remote desktop connections in Windows XP.

TERMINAL SERVICES AND REMOTE DESKTOP
Although Remote Desktop uses the Terminal Services service, it doesn't require the Terminal Services component, and the Terminal Services component enables remote clients to connect to a server and execute applications.

Enabling Remote Desktop

The Remote Desktop system is administered through the System control panel, shown in Figure 4.12. To enable remote administration, click Allow Users to Connect Remotely to This Computer within the Remote Desktop section of the control panel.

You can restrict remote desktop connections to specific users by clicking the Select Remote Users button. The Administrator (and members of the Administrators group) always has access to the machine remotely once Remote Desktop has been enabled, but other users do not. Because we're enabling it specifically for remote administration of IIS, allowing other users to access it is not a good idea.

Connecting Through Remote Desktop Connection

To connect to a server with Remote Desktop enabled, use the Remote Desktop Connection application within the Accessories, Communication section of the Start menu. This is installed by default on Windows Server 2003 and Windows XP machines, or you can install the RDC Client from the Windows Server 2003 CD or download it from Microsoft. Just as if logging in locally, you will need to provide a login and password and, if necessary, an alternative domain.

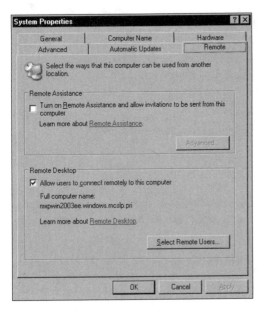

FIGURE 4.12   Enabling Remote Desktop.

Once connected, the interface and environment will seem disturbingly familiar. In fact, you can see in Figure 4.13 that aside from the addition of the RDC status bar, the environment is exactly the same.

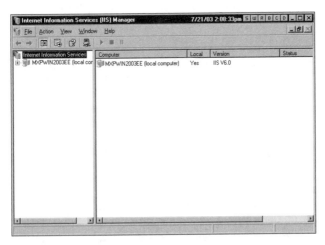

FIGURE 4.13   Managing a remote machine through the Remote Desktop Connection.

Within an RDC connection, you can do anything that you can do when working on the console—albeit often at a reduced speed. The interface, tools, and everything else is the same—and unlike the IIS Manager remote administration and Web Administration systems you can change the other, non-IIS related configurations too.

Connecting Through the Web

Although Remote Desktop Connection is supported over Internet and by a variety of clients (including Mac OS/Mac OS X, all Windows versions, and even the PocketPC/Windows Mobile platform), there are times when you only have access to the Web.

As we've seen, the Web administration interface is extensive but isn't able to do everything. Using the Remote Desktop Connection system, we can connect to the server through a Web connection and still gain full access to the remote desktop.

To enable this functionality, it must have been installed within the IIS system. You can check or enable this service using the Add/Remove Programs control panel and the Add/Remove Windows Components applet.

Expand Application Server, Internet Information Services, World Wide Web Service and check the Remote Desktop Web Connection. You might be asked for your CD as Windows updates the components.

Once the system has been installed, open a Web browser on any machine and type in a URL of the form http://myservername/tsweb, where myservername is the name of the machine on which you installed the Remote Desktop Web Connection component. You should get a window similar to the one shown in Figure 4.14.

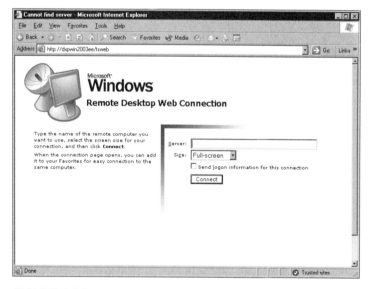

FIGURE 4.14 Opening a remote desktop connection through the Web.

One of the interesting things about the Remote Desktop Web Connection is that once it's installed on one machine, it provides you with access to any machine running RDC—the Web site is merely a jump point for loading the ActiveX control that provides support for RDC. This means that you can install it on a gateway server and still access the rest of your network, without installing RDWC on every machine.

You can also choose, through the Web interface, the size of the desktop you want to open to the remote server. Normally this information is sent automatically from the client. If you opt to send login information, it uses the credentials that apply with your current Web connection, using integrated Windows authentication if your client is able to supply the information.

Again, once connected, everything is just the same as with the standard RDC client or directly on the console.

WEB-BASED RDC

It catches quite a few folk out, so be aware that the Web-based RDC client doesn't operate over port 80. Instead, it works over the standard RDC port (default is 3389). Only the ActiveX component loaded from the Web interface is actually sourced over port 80. This is important because if you have a firewall at your location that filters out everything but port 80 traffic, your RDC system isn't going to work. If you want to open up port 3389 on your firewall, remember to specify source and destination IP addresses or at least ranges if you can.

Advanced Logging

Nobody likes looking through the Web logs generated by IIS, or any other Web server for that matter, but being able to extract useful information from them is as important as having the site running in the first place. The better the quality of your logs, the more information you can obtain.

However, there is generally a trade-off between what can be useful to record and the impact of the additional information on the performance of the server. For example, thinking about some basic information that you might record, such as the date, time, URL accessed, and the status code, it could easily be 250 or more bytes of information. On a busy server, that could be many KB every second and could even approach MB over a period of a few hours.

IIS 6 incorporates a number of improvements in the logging system, but the main one is the new binary logging format, which can have a dramatic impact on server performance.

Log File Content Improvements

IIS 6 incorporates a few content improvements to resolve limitations in the previous versions. The most significant of these is the addition of UTF-8 support for multi-byte and extended character sets.

UTF-8 Logging

With international sites, chances are that you will be dealing with extended character sets and quite possibly multi-byte characters such as Kanji. With previous versions of IIS, log files would be written using the standard ASCII format, making it difficult to identify specific pages and URLs accessed.

IIS 6 will now write log files using the UTF-8 character set. Like binary logging though, it's a global property—it's either on for the entire IIS installation or it's off.

To set the property, right-click on the machine on which you want to enable UTF-8 logging and select Properties from the pop-up list to show the IIS computer properties as seen in Figure 4.15.

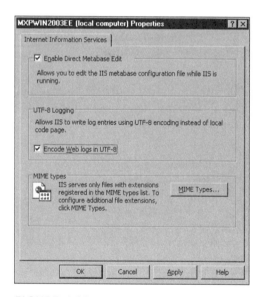

FIGURE 4.15   Configuring UTF-8 logging.

Check (or uncheck) the Encode Web Logs in UTF-8 check box. You must restart IIS in order for the changes to take effect—you can either let IIS Manager do this for you, or you can do it manually at a more suitable time.

HTTP Sub-status Codes

IIS 6 now records the sub-status code for a request, as opposed to just the main status code. For example, an authorization failure because of an ACL problem would be logged as a 401 error under IIS 5 and earlier. Within IIS 6, it would be logged as a 401.3 error. This makes it significantly easier to trace problems and identify issues raised by users.

SSL Statistics

A very small change that might affect some site statistics is that IIS 6 records the number of decrypted bytes during SSL communication, rather than the IIS 5.1 and earlier method of recording only the number of bytes transferred.

Binary Log File Format

Binary logging uses a fixed binary format for the storage or log information. There are a number of benefits to this. First, it's significantly more efficient—fields such as the date and time can be stored within a couple of bytes, compared to the 10–15 used in the W3C, IIS, or NCSA formatted logs.

This also has a domino effect on the performance—IIS buffers 64KB of log information before writing it to disk. With text-based logs, that buffer will fill more rapidly. With binary logging, it will take a lot longer, meaning fewer log writes and a lower overall overhead of the IIS service.

The downside is that we can't just open the file and view the contents; it needs to be specially parsed to extract the information from it. This also means that we can't just join log files together to produce larger logs for processing without going through the conversion process first.

Binary logging is also a global property—either all sites (including FTP and HTTP sites) are logged using the binary method, or individual sites are logged using one of the various text formats.

Enabling Binary Logging

To enable centralized binary logging, you must set a property within the Metabase—it can't be done through IIS manager. The path to the property is /LM/W3SVC/CentralBinaryLoggingEnabled, which is a simple binary value (stored in a DWORD type), where true enables binary logging.

There are a number of ways you can do this, including editing the raw XML or using the Metabase Explorer tool from the resource kit. The suggested way, though, is through the adsutil.vbs script:

```
cscript adsutil.vbs SET W3SVC/CentralBinaryLoggingEnabled true
```

Once set, you will need to restart IIS, which is easier done from here if we're already at the command line:

```
net stop W3SVC

net start W3SVC
```

Once IIS has restarted, information will be placed into the binary log file, with an extension of .ibl (so that it's not recognized as a text file by default). Unless you've otherwise changed the location of your log files, they will be placed in to the %systemroot%\System32\Logfiles\ W3SVC directory.

If you want to change the directory or log renewing parameters, changing the Metabase is the easiest way to change them. Look within the /LM/W3SVC tree for properties starting with 'Log'.

Parsing Binary Log Files

You can't read binary log files directly—well, you can open them in a text editor, but you probably won't make a lot of sense out of the contents.

The format of the files is basically a chain or fixed length records generated in the form of a structure within C/C++ or Visual Basic. The MSDN site has details on the exact format of these files.

A better solution is to use one of the existing tools, such as Seagate Crystal Reports, WebTrends, or Analog. The binary format is, in fact, a recognized standard called Internet Binary Logging (hence the .ibl extension) and is readable by many of the log parsing and reporting utilities.

Converting Binary Log Files

If your chosen log processing tool doesn't support the IBL format or you want to be able to browse the contents through a standard text editor, you will need to convert the binary into a text format.

The convlog file, which has been a part of Windows for some time, doesn't support the IBL format, but the Resource Kit comes with Log Parser, which can read these and many other formats. As well as being a general purpose parsing tool that can generate summary information and search for specific patterns within a log file, Log Parser can also convert files between the different formats.

Log Parser supports two output formats when converting binary files—the W3C Extended Format and the native IIS format. To use Log Parser in this way from the command line, you must use the -c command-line option and then specify the input format (using the -i option) and the output format (-o). For example, to convert all the entries in a binary file to W3C format, you might use

```
logparser -c -i:BIN -o:W3C input.ibl output.log
```

Because Log Parser can also understand and filter the contents, we can also apply filters to the generated text file. For example, to get all the 404 errors from a file

```
logparser -c -i:BIN -o:W3C input.ibl output.log "StatusCode==404"
```

Binary logs contain all the log information for all the Web sites on a single server, but you can split it into separate, site-based log files by doing two things. First, use a wildcard in your output destination, and second, switch on the multisite option.

For example, we can change our original conversion line to

```
logparser -c -i:BIN -o:W3C input.ibl W3SVC*\output.log -multisite:on
```

Check the documentation for some additional information on how to use Log Parser for parsing and converting log files.

Centralized (Remote) Logging

You can go one stage further in the centralization process with IIS 6 by configuring individual logs to be written to the same central server through a UNC share. You can do this, for example, to introduce a single server for monitoring purposes (perhaps combining it with System Monitor or Network Monitor functionality).

There is a trade-off here, though. Using this method obviously increases your network use and will have a performance hit on your IIS servers because the time taken to write to the network is longer than that to write to a local disk.

If you are using a secondary network segment to support the 'background' network chatter between your servers and domain controllers, separate from the client-side network segment, this can go some way to alleviating the problem. But be prepared to suffer some performance hit for the benefit of centralizing your logging.

> **NETWORK SECURITY**
> Whether on a private or public segment, the information will still be sent to the server in unencrypted format. For security, consider enabling IPSec between the IIS servers and the logging server.

To enable logging using this method, create a shared directory onto which the log files will be kept on a server. I also recommend that you create a directory within the share for each server that you expect to log in this way. Then right-click on the Web Site's folder within IIS and choose Properties. Now click Properties within the Enable Logging section and enter the UNC location of the share you want to use in the Log File Directory area.

On the server, log files will be created within the directory you specified, with a separate directory (of the form W3SVC#, where # is the site identifier) for each site.

Performance and Reliability

5

IN THIS CHAPTER

- ▶ **Improvements in content caching** 99
- ▶ **Worker Process Enhancements** 102
- ▶ **Defining Quality of Service** 104

What's New

The performance and speed of your Web sites should always be a concern. This is actually the primary reason behind what must be the biggest change in the way IIS operates—the new execution model. We actually looked at this in greater detail in Chapter 2, "Architecture and Execution." We can summarize the key points as

- **Increased performance**—The separation of the component that accepts requests and the one that processes them enables IIS 6 to more efficiently handle and respond to requests. This is especially true on systems that have multiple processors because individual CPUs can be used to handle specific sites or applications according to the configuration. This makes it more efficient to run multiple sites on a single machine.

- **Greater stability**—By separating the worker process and request handler components, IIS 6 can control the worker processes without affecting how new requests are accepted. In fact, IIS 6 can be made to automatically restart worker processes at set intervals, memory, or CPU limits. It can even shut down and re-create worker processes if they are found to be using up too many resources or they have crashed. This helps keep your sites up and running without administrator intervention, improving the overall performance and throughput of the server.

- **Greater control**—Because the system is split and responses are handled by application pools, we can control and limit applications and Web sites more easily. We can limit individual site capacity, give priority to specific sites, and allocate specific sites to a specific class or group of worker processes.

- **Improved scalability**—Because resources for processing sites are allocated dynamically as they are needed, rather than the pre-IIS 6 method of pre-allocating resources for potential use, IIS 6 is capable of handling more Web sites. Not only can worker processes be generated dynamically because the HTTP.sys driver is separate from the processing system, but it can also be listening for requests even when worker processes aren't running.

However, this isn't the end of the new performance features built into IIS. To improve communication performance, IIS can compress responses back to clients. In IIS 6, we gain greater control over what items can be compressed.

IIS 6 also enables us to define quality of service (QoS) parameters to help us tune the performance of our Web site and dynamic components.

Caching information is just another way in which we can improve the performance of our Web sites. Caching is not new, but IIS 6 incorporates a number of improvements, both in the response mechanism and the way in which it caches information internally ready for supply to a client. In some instances, the content can be returned by the HTTP.sys kernel mode driver without having to use a worker process to handle the request.

We're going to be looking at all these issues in this chapter and also one that you might not associate with performance—the issue of patch management. Keeping your machine up and running is ultimately what performance is all about, and updating your machine is a task that can temporary disable your site, reducing its performance.

Asynchronous CGI

In the past, common gateway interface (CGI) applications have been loaded by IIS on an individual basis. The main reason for this was security and stability. Although an ISAPI could be loaded into its own separate memory space and be relatively safe, CGI applications were seen as unknown quantities.

For some sites and extensions, this caused a bottleneck because the only way to support a CGI script was through this single execution model system. Some traditionally CGI-based systems, such as Perl, got around this by producing an ISAPI alternative for running Perl scripts.

However, for non-ISAPI solutions, the problem remained. IIS 6 has removed this restriction by enabling CGI applications to be loaded and executed simultaneously. The worker process model supports this functionality—because each worker process is seen as an isolated solution and can be individually monitored and restarted, the dangers of executing CGI scripts have been eliminated. Meanwhile, the performance of this model has improved.

Site Driven Management

A simple, but effective, way of improving the performance of a server and the sites it supports is to make the management easier. With IIS 5 and earlier, there were two basic modes of operation for the IIS service—either it was on, or it was off.

Unfortunately, even sites that were unaffected by any of the configuration, content, or script changes would be shut down while the update took place.

In IIS 6, Web sites can be taken down individually (as they could in IIS 5). If your site is composed of static and dynamic components, you can also take down individual application pools while you update the dynamic components and leave the static elements available to clients.

To take down a site, rather than the entire server, just right-click on the Web site in IIS Manager and pause or stop the site.

Content Caching

Busy sites often consist of a number of different components and pages that are supplied to the clients. Often, many of these components are the same. For example, static images and HTML page elements are often sent back to a client a number of times, but it doesn't make sense to keep reading the raw content of these files and sending it to clients each time.

Instead, this information can be retrieved from memory if the file has been requested a number of times. IIS 6 improves on the original model by also taking into account how the pages are accessed over the range of a site, dynamically adjusting the cache contents according to site usage.

IIS also improves other areas of the caching process. ISAPI filters can still be cached in memory, just as they could in IIS 5. Other improvements in IIS 6 affect the way ASP content is cached and how the static data caching system works.

Irrespective of the item being cached, IIS 6 can now be configured to use as much as 64GB of memory for the cache. This should be more than adequate to hold the information for most very large sites or a high number of smaller ones, although you will obviously need a fairly significant piece of hardware to support that.

ASP Content

In IIS 5, ASP pages were compiled and executed with the compiled versions stored in memory. This enabled frequently requested pages to be sent back from memory. However, if clients visited a number of pages, it was possible for some of these pages to be removed from the cache before they were actually used.

IIS 6 still executes ASP pages in the same way, and it still keeps a copy of the compiled version in memory. The difference is that it also keeps a copy of the compiled version in memory and, if necessary, stores it on disk as well. Now if an item drops out of the memory cache, IIS can still load a ready-compiled version from the disk, which is quicker than reading the original and re-executing and compiling it.

Actually, the rules are a bit stricter on this. ASP templates are stored on disk only when the memory cache is full. Also, an ASP page should have been accessed at least twice before it is considered for the disk cache.

 CACHING IS NOT COMPILING

Don't mistake ASP template caching for the more efficient and speedier just-in-time compilation that ASP.NET uses. ASP.NET basically compiles pages to binary code, whereas ASP pages are still interpreted more or less line by line.

You can control how many files are cached and stored and where they are cached and stored through the Metabase or through IIS Manager. The Metabase parameters can be set on a Web server, site, directory, or virtual directory and include

- **AspBufferingOn**—This enables or disables ASP buffering—the act of storing the output from an ASP execution in memory before sending to a client. The default is set to true. If set to false, the output is sent directly to the client as it becomes available. This can actually reduce performance by placing more loading on the management of the response.

- **AspScriptEngineCacheMax**—Specifies the maximum number of scripting engines that ASP pages keep cached in memory. By increasing this number, you can improve performance by caching more of the templates in memory. The default is 120.

- **AspScriptFileCacheSize**—Specifies the number of precompiled script files to store in the in-memory ASP template cache. A value of 0 disables the cache (not recommend), -1 caches all pages, and any other positive value specifies the size. The default value is 500.

■ **AspMaxDiskTemplateCacheFiles**—Specifies the maximum number of files that can be stored in the disk cache. The default value is 4294967295, which Windows actually uses to specify an unlimited number (although 4.3 billion seems pretty unlimited already). Any number below this limits it to that size.

■ **AspDiskTemplateCacheDirectory**—The location in which the disk cache of the files will be stored. The default value is %systemroot%\systemroot\inetsrv\ASP Compiled Templates.

If you want to monitor the performance of the template cache, you can use the Templates Cached performance counter. This was also available in IIS 5 and counts the number of cached ASP files both on disk and in memory. To get statistics only on those in memory, use the AspInMemoryTemplatesCached counter.

To control the ASP caching parameters within IIS Manager, use the Cache Options tab (available by right-clicking on the Web Site folder, choosing Properties and then clicking on the Configuration button within the Home Directory panel). You can see an example of the configuration window in Figure 5.1.

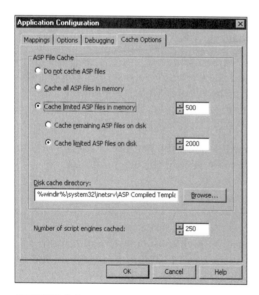

FIGURE 5.1   Changing ASP caching parameters.

The configurable properties match those listed previously in the metabase descriptions. However, some are controlled by a number of entries—the AspScriptFileCacheSize, for example.

Static Content

It seems a little wasteful to constantly use a worker process to process the request for a static element if it already exists in the cache. So IIS 6 doesn't use a worker process for this purpose.

Instead, the HTTP.sys kernel mode driver's role is to respond with the contents of static data if it exists in the in-memory cache of static information. Only if the item in question is not in the cache is a worker process brought into play.

The system can do this because the HTTP.sys driver cannot technically access the file system (mostly for security and performance reasons), but it can access the shared memory used to store cached data.

The actual cache itself is still configured and managed by the registry parameters rather than the Metabase.

Worker Process Enhancements

The combination of the new HTTP.sys kernel mode driver and the use of worker processes to actually handle requests has led to a number of enhancements to the overall performance of the system. We've already looked at many of these here and in earlier chapters.

Overall, the benefits of the new execution model and the worker process system account for more than 80% of the performance improvements in the system. Microsoft predicts a 100% performance increase for most sites when moving to the new model on an 8-way multi-processor machine.

To make the best use of the new architecture, we need to make the best use of the application pool system. Two systems can help improve the overall quality of the worker process system—Web gardens and CPU affinity.

Web Gardens

Web gardens are where you configure a single application pool to use more than just one worker process to handle requests. Modern processors are capable of doing more than one thing at the same time, but you need to be careful about how you configure Web gardens, based on the sites and server you are supporting.

The major benefits from Web gardens only really become apparent on systems with multiple CPUs. For example, in a system configured with only one application pool and one processor, you are unlikely to gain any benefit from using multiple worker processes.

In a two-way SMP system with only one application, you will be able to increase overall throughput by starting two worker processes, one for each CPU, where you will obtain a potential 100% increase in throughput by allowing both processors to process requests.

In the same two-way SMP system with two application pools, you could configure each pool with only one worker process—one for each CPU.

The reality, of course, is that even one worker process is probably not going to saturate your CPU. So many other factors—that is, waiting on data, disk access, and responses from a remote database— mean that a single worker process on even a single processor machine will never achieve its full potential.

Therefore, setting up a Web garden needs careful monitoring of the load on the server to determine how much CPU availability there is and what the limits are for the hardware in question. The more dynamic elements (ASP/ASP.NET) you have in your sites, the more likely you are to benefit for multiple worker processes.

 WEB RESOURCE

For more information on monitoring the performance of IIS, go to Delta Guide series Web site at www.deltaguideseries.com and enter article ID# **A020501**.

WORKER PROCESS SETUP

Generally, I prefer to use at least two worker processes for each application pool, mostly to provide an up-and-running backup worker process in case of a problem with the other one. I've actually found that I get the best performance out of a PIII 833MHz, dual-processor machine when I have eight active worker processes handling a site that is about 50/50 static and template data.

CPU Affinity

CPU affinity is connected to the idea of Web gardens. It enables you to assign a particular application pool to be executed on only one CPU. You can use this to evenly spread your worker processes across your CPUs or to make use of specific functionality in a CPU for particular tasks. For example, a heavy computational process will execute faster on a processor with more level 2 cache than a similarly rated companion.

As an extension of this, IIS 6 has been written with processor affinity in mind, which means that it can take advantage of the single-CPU execution model to get the best performance out of applications. It does this by using the facilities within the CPU to keep as much information as possible within the CPU cache and through the use of consistent registers within the CPU to help increase performance.

This also helps retain the increase in speeds experienced as you raise the number of processors. Instead of spreading the load out across each CPU as it's added to the system, processes continue to run within the confines of their own processor. Additional processors are therefore freely available for additional worker processes.

To set processor affinity, you must set an affinity mask on the application pool to define which processors the application pool can be executed on. To do this, first set the SMPAffinitized property within the metabase. Then set the value of the SMPPRocessorAffinityMask for each application pool. A value of 0 indicates that the pool can execute on any processor.

 BE CAREFUL WITH PROCESSOR AFFINITY

If you decide to set processor affinity, be sure that other administrators in your organization are aware of your new configuration. That way, they won't mistakenly reconfigure IIS or other applications and mess up your manual balance of the processors' workload.

Quality of Service Parameters

The Quality of Service (QoS) parameters are really just a collective term for all the different configurable elements of the IIS system that can be used to improve performance, particularly on a site-by-site basis.

The idea of the QoS system is to enable you to allot specific applications and Web sites with a set of service parameters. For example, if your server hosts a number of Web sites, you might want to tailor your performance parameters to give specific service levels and priorities to a given site so that you can provide a service level of quality.

This involves fine-tuning the various systems so that you can allocate the site specific amounts of CPU time (or even specific CPUs), memory, and bandwidth.

IIS 6 has collected a number of new and existing configurable elements to produce the list of QoS parameters. They are

- Limiting Connections

- Setting Connection Timeouts

- Utilizing HTTP Compression

- Throttling Bandwidth

- Enabling HTTP Keep-alives

- Enabling CPU Monitoring

- Configuring Application Pool Queue Length Limits

Some of this isn't new—many of these items were available in past versions of IIS. What is new is how some of these items are configured (including new parameters) and how this affects processing as a whole. Information about these areas is given next—with links to additional information or chapters where appropriate.

Limiting Connections

You've been able to limit the number of simultaneous connections in IIS 4, IIS 5, and now in IIS 6. The purpose of the connection limit is to prevent your machine from being bombarded by hundreds or thousands of connections—each of which must be processed. Setting the limit to high or not enabling it can lead to your machine being swamped. Setting it too low might reject users whose requests could be processed.

In a QoS environment, we can use the connection throttling to limit connectivity to individual sites while giving higher unlimited connection limits to other more important sites.

To limit the number of connections

1. Open the properties for the Web Sites to set global properties or the properties for a specific Web site to limit the settings to just one site.

2. Change to the Performance tab.

3. Click the Connections Limited To option and adjust the number to the limit you desire.

You can also limit by bandwidth, which is covered later in this section.

Setting Connection Timeouts

Connection timeouts help you control your resources by freeing up connections that might otherwise have died or failed during communication. These failed connections use up slots that could be employed for genuine requests and responses.

The default setting of 120 seconds is quite long. Setting a value of 15 or 30 seconds might be more appropriate. Set the value too low, and the connection might be dropped before the request or the response has been completed, even on a perfect connection.

To set connection limits

1. Open the properties for the Web Sites to set global properties or the properties for a specific Web site to limit the settings to just one site.

2. On the Web Site tab, adjust the value of the Connection Timeout.

KEEP-ALIVES

The Keep Alive functionality is linked to the timeout value—connections are only kept alive for as long as the timeout value. So don't adjust it too low, or your server will take a performance hit through having to open and handle a larger number of connections.

The `ConnectionTimeout` property in the metabase can also be used to set this value and is a replacement for the previous `ServerListenTimeout` property. The `MinFileBytesPerSec` property has also been added. This determines the length of time the client has to receive the entire response. The timeout value for shutting down a connection is calculated by dividing the size of the entire response (including the header information) by the MinFileBytesPerSec property to determine the maximum allowable response time period (the ConnectionTimeout property).

So, a response of 32K with a MinFileBytesPerSec value of 2048 would be given 16 seconds to accept the response. The default value is 240 bytes per second.

Utilizing HTTP Compression

Text file transfers—particularly HTML—from your server to your clients can dramatically increase the performance of your server by making more efficient use of the available band-width. This means that requests are completed quicker, freeing up the resources and allowing the server to process more requests.

Sure, we get a slight performance hit because of the compression, but on a text heavy Web site, the increase in request processing outweighs the decrease in processor availability.

Two different entities can be compressed—static files and script responses. Both are initially compressed on-the-fly, and then a compressed version is stored in a temporary directory to be used next time, just like a typical cache.

To enable compression

1. Open the properties for the Web Sites to set global properties.

2. Change to the Service tab (see Figure 5.2).

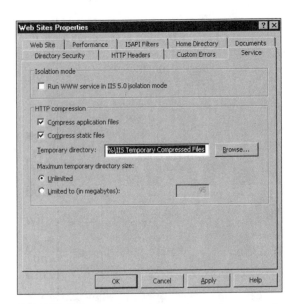

FIGURE 5.2 Setting response compression parameters.

3. In the HTTP compression section, select whether to compress application files or static files.

4. In the Temporary Directory box, specify the location of the directory used to store compressed files. The default directory should be fine for most sites, or you can specify an alternative. However, it must be on an NTFS partition.

5. You can limit the amount of space allocated for the compressed file cache by selecting the Limited To (in Megabytes) option and setting the value `Maximum temporary directory size`.

 WEB RESOURCE

For more information on how compression works, go to the Delta Guide series Web site at www.deltaguideseries.com and enter article ID# **A020502**.

Throttling Bandwidth

The throttling of connections and of bandwidth are closely related. The bandwidth throttling limits the transfer rate for communication for a given Web site. This can work with connection throttling to reduce or limit the available request processing power for a site, or it can be used as an alternative method to restrict the bandwidth allocated to an entire server.

To set the bandwidth throttle for a server or Web site

1. Open the properties for the Web Sites to set global properties or the properties for a specific Web site to limit the settings to just one site.

2. Click the Performance tab (see Figure 5.3).

3. In the Bandwidth Throttling section, select the Limit the Total Network Bandwidth Available for All Web Sites on this Server check box if you are setting preferences for the entire server, or check the Limit the Network Bandwidth Available to This Web Site box for a single site.

4. Specify the Maximum Bandwidth for the server or site.

Enabling HTTP Keep-Alives

A typical Web site access doesn't consist of one hit and one request. Web pages have graphics, which will also be loaded from the same site. If your visitor decides to stay, she also travels around your site looking at other pages.

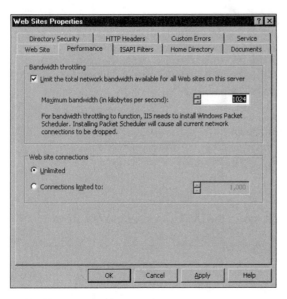

FIGURE 5.3   Throttling the bandwidth allocated to a server.

Continuing to open, read, write, and close a connection for each access would be incredibly wasteful, so connections can be 'kept alive' so that in many cases a single page can be processed with a single open connection and multiple request/response exchanges.

To enable Keep-alives

1. Open the properties for the Web Sites to set global properties or the properties for a specific Web site to limit the settings to just one site.

2. On the Web Site tab, check the Enable HTTP Keep-alives to enable and uncheck to disable.

Note that Keep-alives do not affect how requests are handled. These are still placed one by one in to the request queue for the appropriate application pool; only the actual connection remains constant.

Enabling CPU Monitoring

CPU monitoring allows IIS (when working in Worker process isolation mode) to monitor the CPU usage and to kill and restart worker processes that are consuming large amounts of CPU time.

▶ For more information on setting the CPU monitoring parameters, **see** Chapter 2, **p. 15**.

Configuring Application Pool Queue Length Limits

The queue length on application pools defines how many requests are waiting to be processed by the worker process in the application pool. Setting this value too high can leave the number of requests so large that the client times out the request before the server has a chance to respond. Setting it too low can reject requests even though there is capacity for the request to be processed.

▶ For more information on setting application pool queue lengths, **see** Chapter 2, **p. 15**.

Network Load Balancing

Network Load Balancing (NLB) enables you to create a group of machines (called an NLB cluster) that are then responsible for processing the requests sent to a single IP address (that is, the one configured for a Web site). Servers choose, more or less by committee, which one of them will process the request, according to availability and loading on each of the servers in the NLB cluster.

NLB was available in Windows 2000, but only for the Advanced Server and Datacenter Server versions. NLB is now supported by all versions of the operating system, so we can use an NLB cluster to help improve performance across two or more servers even when running the Web Edition.

Patch Management

Keeping your machines up-to-date should help keep them in tip-top condition and therefore at the highest performance. It should also ensure that any known chinks in the stability and the security of IIS should have been fixed so that you can keep your Web site running at full speed. In previous versions of IIS, any patches or updates had to be applied while IIS was disabled. Because of the new worker process model, patches can be installed while IIS is running with the worker processes simply recycled at the end.

Windows Server 2003 also incorporates the Windows Update functionality. This provides an automatic system for critical updates and security hot fixes. This enables each machine to either

- Notify you when a patch is available

- Download the patch and notify you

- Download and install the patch at a scheduled time

You can see the options in Figure 5.4.

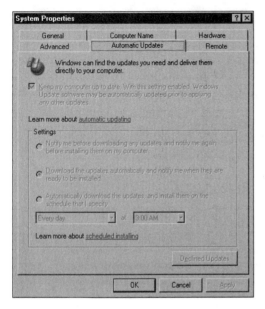

FIGURE 5.4   Setting automatic update parameters.

For an enterprisewide solution, you can use Software Update Services to download the updates for an entire network and then distribute them to your servers and clients. You also get to approve updates before they are distributed to your clients.

Development and Deployment

What's New

IIS 6 has a lot more than just a new execution environment, security, and performance improvements. Without support for actually deploying and developing Web sites, IIS would be nothing more than a file exchange platform.

The Microsoft .NET Framework has heralded a number of significant changes in the way applications are developed and deployed. The .NET system is compatible with a wide array of languages and has a rich class framework for easier development, as well as support for key components of the modern Web application, such as support for Web services; something we'll look at in this chapter.

A couple of items have been covered elsewhere that also affect the way in which ASP.NET applications are executed within IIS 6, including

- Faster execution—ASP.NET applications are compiled, and their compiled forms are stored, both in memory and on disk, eliminating the need to recompile the ASP code each time it is accessed if it has already left the cache.

- Memory, deadlock, and crash protection—Through the worker process system, it's much easier to control and recover from problems when executing an ASP component. Worker processes can be automatically restarted when a problem has been identified or recycled based on time, request, CPU or memory limits.

In this chapter, we're going to have a quick look at the main components, elements, and support when developing and deploying applications within IIS 6. We'll also look at the supported languages, the impact of the .NET Framework, and some of the ISAPI extensions that allow programmers to better control and respond to their environment.

 .NET FRAMEWORK AND IIS ADMINISTRATION

If you're like me, and most other administrators, the sight of the phrase ".NET Framework" makes your eyes glaze over. Developer stuff, right? But stick with it, the Framework includes security management and a number of other factors that are well within the realm of Windows and IIS administration.

ISAPI Extensions

IIS 6 has also improved certain elements of the underlying scripting and IIS integration. The custom error system is a part of this extension, but there are additional components that enable closer integration and cooperation between IIS and any scripts you are running.

The majority of these extensions are designed to improve the overall performance of your Web applications, whether that's actual throughput or it solves a previously complex problem.

Request Redirection (ExecuteURL)

Redirection is commonly used to redirect a user to an alternative page when a page has moved. With a new ISAPI extension, HSE_REQ_EXEC_URL, you can now redirect requests directly from within an application to another URL.

The redirection is not like the static redirection, but it is essentially equivalent to re-executing the request through an alternative URL. You can use this to chain ISPAI filters together to achieve a specific result.

For example, you might want to chain the basic application request, a formatting request, and a template request together—each using a different ISAPI filter. This used to require the production of a raw data reading ISAPI filter—in IIS 6 we can do this by calling the ExecuteURL function to pass off the output from the current, processed, request to another URL.

Wildcard Application Maps

Typically, the extension of a file in a request is used by IIS to determine which CGI application or ISAPI filter is used to process it. For example, a file with an .asp extension is an ASP script, whereas .pl is a Perl CGI and .plx is a Perl ISAPI document.

The problem with this approach is that it means that all elements within your site need to have a specific extension to allow them to run. If you want multiple extensions to parse the same document through the same ISAPI filter or CGI script, you have to set them up individually. It's also impossible to have all documents parsed by a specific filter, irrespective of their extension.

In IIS 6 you can create a wildcard application map—this maps all files matching a particular wildcard specification to an ISAPI filter. In turn, this enables you to automatically parse all content through an ISAPI filter. Used in combination with the ExecuteURL feature, it means that you can parse a request, and then use ExecuteURL to redirect the actual request on to a handler.

This can be used in a variety of environments where pre-parsing of the requested documents further aids the actual request. For example, in a banking or e-commerce site, you might use this to authenticate users before redistributing the request to the correct script to handle the actual response.

For another example of where this can be used, imagine a download site that enables you to download copies of a document in a variety of formats. Rather than keeping fixed copies of the document in the directory in all the different formats, you could create a wildcard application map that points to an ISAPI filter that builds the document dynamically.

When a user requests the report.html file, the wildcard request redirects the request to your ISAPI application, which then uses ExecuteURL to run the HTML generation and return the document in HTML format. When the user requests the report.doc, the same systems uses ExecuteURL to run the Microsoft Word document script.

Although we could do this by using a script and parameters to the script, using such a system makes it difficult to publicize specific URLs without making them complex—that is, http://www.mycompany.com/report.doc is much easier to enter and remember than http://www.mycompany.com/docrequest.asp?name=report&format=doc.

You configure the wildcard mapping settings through the Application Configuration dialog box (see Figure 6.1).

To get to this dialog box, use the following steps:

1. Right-click the Web site or virtual directory that you want, and then click Properties.

2. Change to the appropriate tab (Home Directory, Virtual Directory, or Directory).

3. In the Application settings area, click Configuration, and then click the Mappings tab.

To install a new wildcard mapping:

1. On the Mappings tab, click Insert. You will get the dialog box seen in Figure 6.2.

2. Type the path to the DLL in the Executable text box or use the Browse button to open a file dialog and find it. Remember to click the Application Engine check box if the DLL is a script engine. Then click OK.

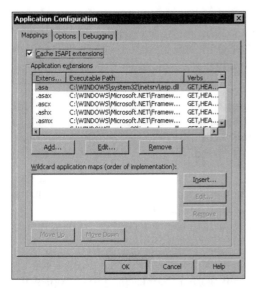

FIGURE 6.1   Application configurations.

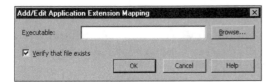

FIGURE 6.2   Application/Extension mappings.

To edit or delete a wildcard application map:

1. In the application extensions list, click the script map that you want to change.

2. Click Edit to alter the script map, or click Remove to remove the script map.

The wildcard system works in a very specific way and is still subject to the same limitations as the rest of the ISAPI filters system. When executing a request, the impact and execution order of the ISAPI filters is as follows:

1. The request is handled by any existing ISAPI filters on the root Web site, in the order in which they appear within the application extensions list.

2. The request is sent to any wildcard application mapped applications, again in the order they appear. If wildcard maps exist at both the directory and site level, only the

directory level maps are applied. If no directory specific maps exist, the site level maps are applied.

3. The extension of the request is used to determine whether any further execution, according to the mapping, is applied through the normal ISAPI or CGI application.

Output Caching

Before IIS 6, if you had multiple buffers of data that needed to be written back to the client (template components, formatted data, generated HTML, and so on), you would have to separately call the WriteClient() function to submit each item back to the client.

With IIS 6, two new features, VectorSend and FinalSend, simplify the process. Now, you can just specify the buffer or file location with calls to VectorSend; this makes the IIS 6 kernel driver aware of the data. When you've completed the sequence, you use FinalSend to signify the end of the data.

This indicates to IIS 6 that the data should be collated and sent back to the client. Because IIS, not the ISAPI filter or application, is responsible for this writing, the worker process can go on to process the next request.

Custom Errors

One of the problems with ASP and other forms of dynamic elements is that you need to handle errors within the application itself. Although this is what you want sometimes—say, an invalid login or empty search results—other times, you want to raise a specific HTTP error.

Through the ExecuteURL system, it's now possible to pass off errors within your applications to the main error handling system within IIS 6, so your users get a consistent error message and view.

Worker Process Restarting

A new ISAPI extension, HSE_REQ_REPORT_UNHEALTHY, can be used by an extension to force the ISAPI application's worker process to be recycled. This is useful if the application has identified that the ISAPI filter has become unstable or unreliable, or if the system enters an unknown state. You can also supply a string that will be written to the Application log to highlight the reason for the error.

RECYCLING
In order for the ISAPI call to actually initiate a recycle operation, health monitoring should be switched on in the application pool configuration. Recycle requests are ignored if health monitoring is not enabled.

COM+ Access

COM+ services are now exposed to the ASP service in a different manor. In previous versions, COM+ services used the WAM object in the COM+ configuration store to use a specific set of services that were to be used with specific COM components.

In IIS 6, COM+ can now be used independently of the COM components, allowing developers to access COM+ services directly.

In addition, the following services have been added since Windows 2000:

- Fusion support—Enables ASP applications to use a specific version of a DLL or COM component. This is useful for backward compatibility with existing applications.

- Partition Support—COM+ partitions can now be assigned a different configuration for different users, instead of a single configuration for a specific application.

- Tracker support—Tracks when code is running within an ASP session; useful for debugging applications.

Development Platforms

Just as important as the built-in support within the ISAPI and deployment environments are the languages compatible with the IIS 6 platform. You have two choices within IIS 6 (and in previous versions)—those available through the ASP/ASP.NET system and those available separately through the CGI and ISAPI filter systems.

The .NET Framework is probably the biggest change in terms of deployment with IIS 6 and provides a number of significant benefits and advances over previous development and deployment options.

Through .NET

The .NET Framework is really a combination of a number of different technologies all designed to work together to provide better cooperation, integration, and faster development times. The basic core of the idea is the use of Internet technologies to enable better cooperation between components and an improvement over the object-based models, such as the Distributed Component Object Model (DCOM).

.NET doesn't replace COM/DCOM (yet), but does make it easier for the components to talk to each other. Languages that support the .NET development environment create code in Intermediate Language (IL). When an application is executed, the IL is used as the basis for the execution.

 **WEB RESOURCE**

For a quick refresher on the .NET Framework, go to the Delta Guide series Web site at www.deltaguideseries.com and enter article ID# **A020601**.

The Common Language Runtime (CLR) is the API that provides the core API for communicating with the different components, such as ADO.NET for database access.

Because the IL accesses the CLR, we have access to the entire suite of .NET functionality from any language that supports .NET and produces IL compatible code. This means that ASP.NET applications can also be written in any .NET supporting language.

At the time of writing (August 2003), more than 25 languages were certified compatible with .NET, including

- Visual Basic/VB.NET

- C/C++

- C# (a new object and .NET aware variation on C)

- Java

- J# (a new .NET aware variation on Java)

- Perl (through the ActivePerl/VisualPerl products from ActiveState)

- Python (through the ActivePython/VisualPython products from ActiveState)

- JScript.NET

With such a wide array of languages available, it should be easy to find developers, easy for the developers to choose the language they prefer to work in, and easy to deploy the application to your servers, regardless of the source language. In fact, in many situations, deploying an ASP.NET application is as simple as copying over the files in question—no additional installation of software or components is required.

Independent Options

Pretty much any language is supported through IIS 6—as in previous versions—through the common gateway interface (CGI). Beyond the standard offerings available through ASP.NET, the most common continue to be supported through IIS 6:

- Perl—This is available in both CGI and ISAPI compatible alternatives through the ActivePerl distribution from ActiveState.

- Python—Also available from ActiveState (as ActivePython) for use with IIS.

- PHP—Available in an ISAPI compatible state from php.net.

Web Services

Web Services aren't strictly a new technology, nor are they new or unique to IIS 6 or, indeed, to Microsoft. That's really part of the point.

Web Services are an architecture and platform neutral method of providing access to services and of exchanging information between clients and servers, as well as between servers while executing a request.

Although Web services are not a new feature, IIS 6 does integrate more fully with the .NET Framework—of which Web service support is a significant component.

 WEB RESOURCE

For a technical overview about how Web services work and will improve the Web development experience, go to the Delta Guide series Web site at www.deltaguideseries.com and enter article ID# **A020602**.

Unicode Support

One of the many problems faced by IIS managers and Web developers is the issue of languages and providing multiple language Web sites for users. The technicalities of providing multiple sites are really beyond the scope of this book, but one element of IIS 6 is important to how you provide these services to your users.

Unicode support is built into IIS 6 in terms of supporting static files, and it's also built into the logging mechanisms so that you can record these transactions. IIS 6 already supports UTF-8 encoded URLs for retrieving files from a Web server.

IIS 6 also allows ISAPI filters to extract server variables in Unicode format and to get to request values and the Unicode representation of the request URL using Unicode.

This should mean that beyond the domain, you can enable and encode all the other elements of your Web site in the native script and language/character set.

Migrating from IIS 4/5 to IIS 6

What's New

The primary objective of this chapter is not to give a summary of everything else in this book—which is essentially a guide to everything that is new in IIS 6, but instead to show you how to upgrade from a previous version of IIS to IIS 6 as quickly and painlessly as possible.

There are, of course, two versions of IIS that most people are going to migrate from—IIS 4 and IIS 5. You might also be upgrading or migrating a Web site from an IIS 5.1 installation on a Windows XP machine to Windows Server 2003.

Whatever the source version, there are essentially two avenues to take when performing the migration. The first is to upgrade your existing machine, and the second is to create a new server and migrate the content.

We'll start off in this chapter by looking at the major differences between IIS 4 and IIS 5 and the new IIS 6. Then we'll look at the upgrade process—that is, upgrading your host operating system from an older Windows NT 4.0 or Windows 2000 server product. This will include a look at the areas in which you will need to make changes after the upgrade to get your machine up and running again.

The upgrade process, though, is not always practical. For starters, it assumes you want to continue running the Web site on the same machine. Often, you will be migrating to new hardware at the same time, and you might also be taking the opportunity to improve the platform, as well as the Web serving environment.

This is where the IIS Migration Tool comes in; it enables you to move an IIS installation from one machine to another, transferring the configuration information and Web site files and data. We'll be taking a closer look at the IIS Migration Tool in this chapter.

The final sections of this chapter concentrate on some specific issues that you might come across after an upgrade has taken place.

Fasttrack Guide—IIS 4 to IIS 6

Listing all the differences between IIS 4 and IIS 6 would require more space than we have in this book—even if we exclude the underlying operating system changes. Of course, a lot of this book is just as applicable to IIS 4 migrations as it is to IIS 5 migrations.

IIS 4 itself was part of the Windows NT 4.0 Option Pack—this was an additional install that added a number of new features to the existing NT 4.0 platform. The primary use of the Option Pack by most people was to upgrade the fairly basic IIS 3 installation to IIS 4.

In fact, IIS development pretty much halted after IIS 4 was released, and even IIS 5 didn't add that many new features to the system. As such, there are really only a few fundamental differences between IIS 4 and IIS 6, and they are the same as those between IIS 5 and IIS 6. It's actually the other components—for example, the extension of management systems and the changes to the IIS management console component—that have any significant effect.

Execution Environment

The biggest difference is obviously the execution environment; something we covered heavily in Chapter 2, "Architecture and Execution." IIS 4 worked with a single process, Inetsrv.exe, which handled the listening and the processing of individual requests.

IIS 6 now separates this into two components—the kernel-side HTTP.sys for listening for connections and the worker processes for actually processing individual requests.

This leads to a number of differences that you need to think about—first, the way that you currently manage your system applications, and how you manage your system performance.

Between IIS 4 and IIS 5, a new type of application pool was created; the Pooled Process enabled a number of applications to be executed within the same shared process space separate from the In Process space of the main Inetsrv.exe application.

With IIS 6, the separation of the connection manager and the processing systems allows you to individually control the two components. This changes the way you manage the server and improves the reliability and the availability of the server.

Supported Services

IIS 6 has extended the number of services supported by the core IIS component. IIS 4 supported only Web (HTTP), Usenet News (NNTP), and FTP services, as well as a minor SMTP forwarding service for handling the distribution of mail from Web forms. IIS 6 now incorporates mail (SMTP) and mailbox (POP3) services, as well.

If you are migrating an existing platform to IIS 6, this shouldn't cause any problems because your existing sites will be migrated as normal. However, you might want to review any additional support services, especially mail servers, in case you can merge existing services.

FrontPage Support

There are some minor differences between the earlier versions of FrontPage and FrontPage 2003 that might break certain elements of the FrontPage code and extensions you are using.

If you are using FrontPage to provide client-based page and site updates, you might want to make use of the WebDAV, which allows users to write HTML straight to the site, either from FrontPage or from other tools such as Word and Excel.

Management

IIS 4 was the first to make extensive use of the Microsoft Management Console (MMC) to provide support for the management interface to the IIS system. You can see an example of this in action in Figure 7.1.

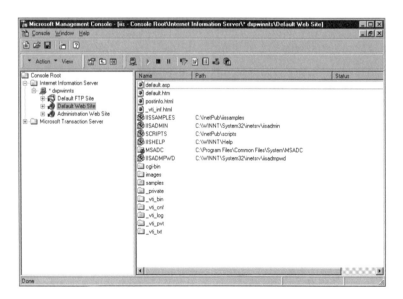

FIGURE 7.1   The IIS MMC snap-in in Windows NT 4.0.

The Internet Service Manager, which would have been installed within the Windows NT 4.0 Option Pack and Microsoft Internet Information Server folders within the Start Menu, is now called IIS Manager and is part of the main Administrative Tools folder.

 WEB RESOURCE

For more information on IIS and the MMC, go to the Delta Guide series Web site at www.delt-aguideseries.com and enter article ID# **A020701**.

In essence, not much has changed in the MMC console, beyond the obvious, but what has expanded is the amount of configurable elements that are controlled directly from within the IIS Manager snap-in to MMC. For example, Web service extensions are directly controlled through the IIS manager.

Also, when working in Worker Process Isolation mode, applications are assigned according to their application pool, and application pools are separately configured within IIS Manager.

Users, Authentication, and Domain Integration

IIS 4 provided some basic integration between the Windows NT domain and IIS, enabling Windows domain authentication to use the Windows NT Domain information. IIS 6 extends the integration to the replacement for Windows NT domains—the Active Directory.

Now, virtually all elements of IIS that require a username are capable of using the Active Directory information.

IIS 6 also incorporates a feature that is part of IIS 5—the capability to automatically authenticate users logged in to an Active Directory domain on their machine to automatically be authenticated and be granted access to directories and applications.

The integration also means that the system is more secure, because data can be secured more effectively through the Active Directory system.

 PASSPORT AUTHENTICATION

IIS 6 also supports Microsoft Passport authentication. However, that's not something you can just turn on, like Windows integrated authentication. It requires yearly fees to Microsoft, additional Web development work, and so forth. Stick with the other levels of authentication for most Web sites.

Fasttrack Guide—IIS 5 to IIS 6

Although there weren't that many differences between IIS 4 and IIS 5, a few items warrant a mention, both in terms of their difference from IIS 4 to IIS 5 and on to IIS 6:

- A slight name change—IIS was Internet Information Server; it became Internet Information Services. The name change reflects the change from a basic Web server to a more generic Internet server.

- Internet Services Manager—This has now become IIS Manager and is part of the Administrative Tools command set.

- Active Directory—Again introduced with IIS 5, it's integration has been further expanded with IIS 6.

- CPU throttling—Introduced in IIS 5 (and as demonstrated in Figure 7.2) this has now been expanded upon. Instead of a single performance tuning element within the Performance tab, it's the worker processes that are used to define the performance characteristics of a given application or site.

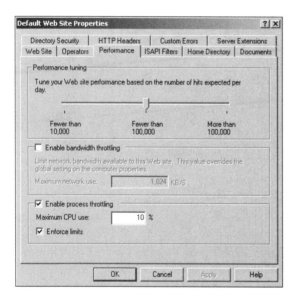

FIGURE 7.2   CPU throttling in IIS 5.

- WebDAV—Support for Web Distributed Authoring and Versioning, which allows clients and applications to edit and update information on a Web site directly and much more easily. It's also a better alternative than using FrontPage.

Feature Comparison (IIS 4 Through IIS 6)

The best way to look at the differences between the systems is actually to compare the various features in a table, which is what I've done in Table 7.1. Rather than concentrating on some isolated features, I've tried to give a well rounded comparison of specific elements within the different versions.

TABLE 7.1 Feature comparison of IIS 4, 5, and 6

Feature	IIS 4	IIS 5	IIS 6
Supported Services			
Web (HTTP)	Yes	Yes	Yes
FTP	Yes	Yes	Yes
SMTP	Limited	Yes	Yes
NNTP	Limited	Yes	Yes
POP3	No	No	Yes
Management Facilities			
MMC	Yes	Yes	Yes
Web	Limited	Limited	Limited
Command line	Limited	Limited	Yes
Programmatic	Limited	Yes	Yes
Direct Metabase Edit	No	No	Yes
Supported Environments			
FrontPage	Yes	Yes	Yes
ASP	Yes	Yes	Yes
ASP.NET	No	Yes	Yes
Perl	Yes	Yes	Yes
Python	Yes	Yes	Yes
PHP	Yes	Yes	Yes
Application Management			
In Process Execution (part of Inetinfo.exe)	Yes	Yes	No
Out of Process Execution	Yes	Yes	Yes
Pooled Process Execution	Yes	Yes	Yes
Automatic Process Management	No	No	Yes
Authentication Support			
Basic Authentication	Yes	Yes	Yes
Anonymous Access	Yes	Yes	Yes
Integrated Windows Authentication	Yes (NT Domains)	Yes (Active Directory)	Yes (Active Directory)
Digest Authentication	No	Yes	Yes
.NET Passport Integration	No	No	Yes
Process/CPU Management			
Hits based throttling	Yes	Yes	Yes
CPU throttling	No	Yes	Yes
Application throttling	No	No	Yes
CPU Affinity	No	No	Yes
Bandwidth throttling	Yes	Yes	Yes

 **FEATURE PARITY**

The most important step in upgrading—and where this chart can help—is in making sure that all the features you require are implemented on IIS 6 and that they're implemented in the same fashion as on your current version of IIS.

Upgrading to IIS 6

IIS 4 was available within Windows NT 4.0 Option Pack for both server and client installations. IIS 4.0 was probably the first version of IIS most people were exposed to as a Web serving solution. Although earlier versions than this exist, it's unlikely you will be using them. IIS 5.0 comes with Windows 2000 server and Professional products.

Upgrading from IIS 4 or IIS 5 to IIS 6 is not as complicated as you might think. The point is that you have to upgrade the operating system to Windows Server 2003—you can't install IIS 6 on your existing Windows NT 4.0 or Windows 2000 server installation.

Upgrades can be completed more or less directly, and they have a number of advantages, such as the capability to upgrade and convert settings directly without further intervention. In many respects, performing an upgrade is the easiest and most effective way of upgrading to IIS 6 without the complexities of the IIS Migration software.

Upgrading also means that sites, locations, static files, data files, and other additional components are kept on the machine; and in many cases, it should be a relatively simple case. What upgrading doesn't do is upgrade anything to do with your site's dynamic elements.

If you are using ASP or VisualBasic components to provide customized information, you're going to need to make some minor modifications to some scripts, depending on what features you have used—it's best to check each script after the upgrade.

Upgrade Compatibility

Your primary concern is going to be the support for the underlying operating systems of Windows Server 2003. The system requirements for Windows Server 2003 are more extensive than Windows NT 4.0, ideally requiring a Pentium III processor running at 500Mhz.

The upgrade paths for Windows Server 2003 Standard Edition are

- Windows NT 4.0 with Service Pack 5 or later

- Windows NT Server 4.0 Terminal Server Edition with Service Pack 5 or later

- Windows 2000 Server

For Windows Server 2003 Enterprise Edition, you can upgrade from

- Windows NT Server 4.0 with Service Pack 5 or later

- Windows NT Server 4.0 Terminal Server Edition with Service Pack 5 or later

- Windows NT Server 4.0 Enterprise Edition with Service Pack 5 or later

- Windows 2000 Server

- Windows 2000 Advanced Server

- Windows Server 2003, Standard Edition

In short, Windows NT 4.0 with Service Pack 5 or Windows 2000 Server platforms can be upgraded to the same platform (basic to Standard editions, or Advanced Server to Enterprise Edition) or better (basic to Enterprise Edition). Note, however, that you can't downgrade—that is, upgrade from Windows 2000 Advanced Server to Windows Server 2003 Standard Edition.

 UPGRADING FROM OTHER OS

If you want to upgrade from an operating system older than Windows NT 4.0, you will need to upgrade to Windows NT 4.0 or later first. If you want to upgrade from a client operating system, the basic rule is that you can't. Certain versions and editions do enable upgrades—for example, Windows 2000 to Windows 2000 Server is possible. Generally, however, it's not recommended.

Also be aware that certain aspects of your Web site and system might not be upgradeable. In particular, custom ISAPI filters and some aspects of your ASP code might not transfer effectively over to your new system.

 TESTING ON WINDOWS SERVER 2003

Even if you are upgrading from a previous version to Windows Server 2003, it's a good idea to test your Web site on IIS 6 before performing the actual upgrade. Although it should be possible to go back to the old Windows NT 4.0 or Windows 2000 installation, if you've got proper backups, it will be much more difficult than changing the new Web site on a new machine.

Upgrade Process

The upgrade process is normally as easy as inserting the Windows Server 2003 CD into your server while it's running and following the onscreen instructions. You can see an upgrade in process in Figure 7.3.

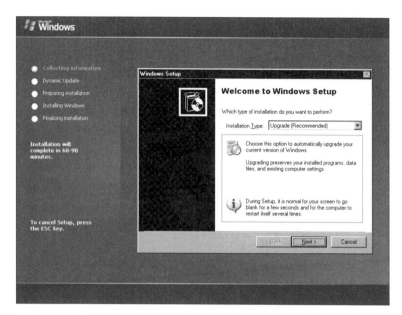

FIGURE 7.3   Upgrading to Windows Server 2003.

However, before you rush to find the installation CD, you need to perform a few bits of preparation:

- Back up your server. Make sure that you have a complete backup that could bring your server back into full service as quickly as possible just in case everything goes wrong.

- Create a separate backup copy of your Web site files, any additional scripts, ISAPI filters, and other components. This will help you move the site to another machine in case the upgrade doesn't work.

- Back up your metabase file. You can find the `metabase.bin` file in `%systemroot%\system32\inetsrv`.

Once you've got the backups (and it's probably a good idea to have backups of the backups), insert the Windows Server 2003 CD and follow the onscreen instructions. Be prepared to wait; the process for upgrading is slightly more complex than a new installation. Whereas a new installation might take 35–45 minutes, an upgrade on the same machine might take 45 minutes to an hour because the installer has to go through a number of checks and verifications to know how to proceed with the upgrade.

For IIS in particular, it will also have to convert the IIS metabase from its binary format into the new XML format and, in the process, translate and convert the Web site definitions and applications into the new model.

After the Upgrade

You are obviously going to notice a few changes, and you will need to make a number of changes after the upgrade process. These include

- Operating mode—IIS 4 installations will be set to execute in IIS 5 Isolation Mode, rather than Worker Process Isolation Mode. IIS 5 Isolation mode is less secure, so you might want to change this. However, doing so might break any applications that you are using, so make sure that you test the system thoroughly before changing over full time to the worker process model.

- IIS availability—If you hadn't made any changes to the default Web site in IIS 4 and IIS 5, IIS won't actually be installed at all during the upgrade. As part of the security implied by Windows Server 2003, default IIS installations are disabled. You probably won't encounter this on a machine that is being upgraded specifically to gain the facilities of IIS 6, but it might if you are upgrading a machine to take the role of a Web/application server.

- Installed Components—ASP and FrontPage will only have been installed and upgraded if you already have these components installed.

- Administration Web Site—The administration site in IIS 4 and IIS 5 will still be there within the default Web site, but it will have been disabled. If you need to have Web-based administration on your new site, you will have to separately install that component.

- Default Web site—The default Web site will still be available, but some of the sub-directories will have been disabled. The Administration site is one example; others include the IIS help (which has been moved to the main Windows help system) and the MSADC Data Connector virtual directory.

The remainder of your Web sites should exist as before, with all their settings and other details intact. Any application pools you had configured in either IIS 4 or IIS 5 will have replicated to an appropriate application configuration under IIS 6. You will have to manually configure these applications with corresponding application pools if you want to convert to the worker process model.

Using the IIS Migration Tool

The IIS Migration Tool is designed to migrate Web sites from one machine to another. It can handle pretty much all source sites, including IIS 4.0, 5.0, and surprisingly 6.0, which can be useful if you want to move a Web site from one machine to another.

MIGRATION TOOL INSTALLATION

The migration tool comes with the IIS 6 Resource kit, which you can download from the Microsoft downloads center at `http://www.Microsoft.com/download`.

The IIS Migration Tool works by running on the destination server—running IIS 6.0—and the source server—running another version of IIS. It's therefore a combination of a migrating and copying tool. You can't use the IIS Migration Tool for migrating content between different versions of IIS on the same machine (which isn't technically possible anyway because the migration tool needs both machines to be working).

The migration tool cannot be used to migrate scripts and filter out all the bugs and problems for migrating from one scripting platform to another. It will migrate the scripts, but it won't fix incompatibilities between the two.

That doesn't make the tool completely useless—for the majority of sites, it's going to do the core work of migrating settings and files. The IIS Migration tool does all the following:

- Backs up the metabase configuration on the target server.

- Migrates the Web site content. You can also copy between different source and destination directories.

- Copies file system access control lists.

 WEB RESOURCE

For more information on IIS and Access Control Lists, go to the Delta Guide series Web site at www.deltaguideseries.com and enter article ID# **A020702**.

- Copies the IIS metabase configuration and migrates the settings between the two servers.

- Maps IIS 4.0 and IIS 5.0 application isolation settings to the new IIS 6.0 application pool settings. What it doesn't do is make your Web site applications IIS 6.0 compatible, nor does it automatically make them Worker Process Isolation mode compatible.

You can also optionally apply the following settings:

- Change the Web root directory path in source files.

- Apply FrontPage Extensions to sites that use FrontPage Server extended sites.

- Change the IP address, port number, and host header (virtual server) to new settings. This is useful if you want to migrate the site to a new server for testing.

Requirements

Before you start, you need to make sure that both your source machine (the one currently holding your site) and the target machine are up and running and configured for network operation.

You also need to ensure that

- IIS is installed and running on both machines. Remember that IIS 6 is not running by default under Windows Server 2003—you must have configured the Application Server Role to install IIS 6.

- The IIS Admin service is running on both machines. You can check this by checking the services. Services was a control panel in Windows NT 4.0 (see Figure 7.4), but is part of the MMC and the Administrative tools folder within Windows 2000 Server and Windows Server 2003. (Figure 7.5 shows the Windows 2000 Services snap-in.)

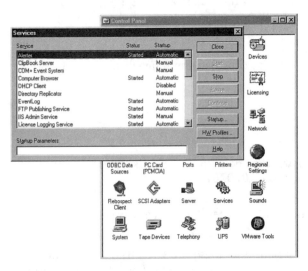

FIGURE 7.4   Services in Windows NT 4.0.

- Administrative file sharing is enabled on the source server. You must have remote access to the administrative file shares for each disk that holds IIS site information, including C$ for the metabase and any additional drives that hold site data. You might need to install/enable the File Sharing component on Windows 2000 to enable this setting.

- You must have administrator privileges for both the source and the target machine.

Finally, remember to have enough space to copy over the source files for the Web site content. Considering the size of disk drives today, this shouldn't be a problem.

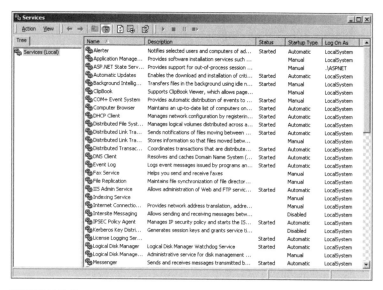

FIGURE 7.5   Services in Windows 2000.

Migrated Items and Limitations

During the migration, the tool migrates all the source data, configuration, and security settings that it is capable of migrating, with a few caveats and exceptions:

- The metabase file is migrated to the new XML format. The source metabase information is backed up by the tool using the location %systemroot%\System32\Inetsrv\Metaback\ IIS Migration Tool Backup.MD##, where ## is an incremental number.

- The following directories and virtual directories are not migrated from IIS 4 and IIS 5:

  - IISSamples

  - IISHelp

  - IISAdmin

  - _vti_bin

  - Printers

  - MSADC

  - IISADMPWD

- Existing directories and files are not overwritten automatically unless you've told the tool to do so. Otherwise, it will prompt to confirm each file/directory to be overwritten during the migration process.

- Data is migrated to the same directory as the source unless you tell it to do otherwise through a command-line option. You cannot migrate the site data to a UNC path unless the UNC path has been mapped to a drive letter—that is, you must write to z:\WWWroot rather than \\WWWFileserver\WWWroot.

- Files from UNC shares on the source will be migrated providing that the current target server can still reach the original UNC share.

- Files and directory security is preserved providing that the machine, domain, and other account identifies can be found within the current security scope.

- Local users are not re-created, and access control lists are not configured for local users after migration. You will need to reset these settings once the migration has completed.

- Server settings (IP address, port number, and host header) are preserved. (Source IPs configured to act on all IP addresses are similarly configured on the destination.) You can change these parameters using a command-line option.

- Application pool settings are migrated according to the following rules:

    - In process applications are placed into an application pool named SourceServerName_InProcess.

    - Pooled applications are placed into an application pool named SourceServerName_Pooled.

    - Isolated applications are placed into a unique application pool called SourceServerName_ApplicationName.

Using the Tool

The migration works through the C$ drive mapping system reading the source configuration, Web site source, and security settings directly from the source file system, re-creating the various settings, migrating the metadata file from its binary format to XML, and then copying over the source files onto the target system.

To use, ideally you need to run it from the command line, although you could start it from the Start->Run system if you want.

The basic syntax for the command is

```
iismt.exe Server Website [options]
```

where Server is the name (or IP address) of the source server you are copying from, and Website is the name or metabase key (W3SVC/1) of the Web site you want to copy.

MIGRATION WORKS ON INDIVIDUAL SITES

You must copy sites individually; you cannot migrate an entire server and all of its Web sites in one go.

This is mildly annoying if you have a lot of Web sites configured, but it also has advantages in that it means we can migrate individual sites to different servers. The site-by-site approach also means that we can migrate a site, test it, and move on to the next, rather than having one big migration and testing phase.

Table 7.2 lists the additional optional command-line parameters and their syntax that you can use.

TABLE 7.2 Migration Tool Command-Line Parameters

Parameter	Description
/user *UserName*	The username to use when communicating with the source server—it should either be a straight `Username` or a domain base `Domain\Username`. If you don't explicitly specify the credentials, the migration tool will attempt to use your current credentials. Note that unless your Active Directory domain is running in mixed compatibility mode, you will need to authenticate with the Windows NT domain.
/password *Password*	The password to go with `Username`.
/path *Path*	The destination directory for the migrated Web site source files. If not specified, it uses the same directory path as on the source server. If you have changed your partition and drive setup so that they do not match the source machine, you will need to use this parameter to set a new location. This parameter is ignored if you are using the /configonly parameter, which doesn't copy site data.
/serverbindings *ServerBindings String*	Sets an alternative IP address, port number, and host header for the Web site during the migration process. The `ServerBindings String` should be in the format `IP:Port:Hostheader`. For example, to change the IP address to use IP address 192.168.1.240, port 8080, and the www.mcslp.com host header, you would use the string `192.168.1.240:8080:www.mcslp.com`. Note that this doesn't actually configure this IP address for the target host. If you don't specify this setting, the migrated Web site will use the default IP address of the target server if the source server also used the default IP address. If the source server specifies an alternate IP address, the alternate IP address will be migrated. Port and host header information is migrated verbatim by default—that is, a site migrated from the default IP address, but on port 8129 and with a host header of mcslp.com, will be migrated to the default IP of the target server with the same port and host header settings.

TABLE 7.2   Continued

Parameter	Description
/siteid *[SiteID]* | Replace	The site ID of the Web site when it is written to the target server. Use this if you want to renumber the sites as they are migrated. If you want to replace an existing site ID number with the migrated site, append the Replace keyword. If you do not specify an alternative site ID during migration, the site ID will simply be the next available number on the target server. If you specify a site ID that already exists on the target server and you have not included the Replace keyword, the migration will fail.
/configonly	Forces the migration tool only to migrate the settings for the site, not the data.
/fpse	Extends a FrontPage Server extended site on the target server if it was running FrontPage Server extensions on the source. Ignored if the /configoly parameter is in effect.
/verbose	Includes additional details of the metabase path copy and file copy stages of the migration process as they occur.
/overwrite	Forces existing files to be overwritten without prompting you beforehand. Without this setting, you will be prompted if a file or directory already exists on the target during the migration process. Best used if a past migration attempt failed and you want to initiate the migration again in a non-interactive session, such as a batch file execution.
/noninteractive	Suppresses messages that prompt the user for input. When this parameter is used, the migration tool exits when it encounters the first error condition. Best used when you are running the migration tool as part of a batch file, but remember to log the output so that you can re-initiate a migration if it fails.

For example, to run the migration tool to migrate the site MCSLP from the server ntiis, you would run the following on the destination server:

```
Iismt.exe ntiis MCSLP
```

To add credentials to the source server and force it to overwrite any existing Web site source files, you would use

```
Iismt.exe ntiis MCSLP /user Administrator /password Pass /overwrite
```

Post Migration

Despite everything that the tool does during the migration process, there will be a few things you will need to do to ensure that your sites are up and running properly again.

In particular,

- Copy additional components—Any DLLs, applications, or other components not located within the Web site source directory will not be copied over. Also, remember that additional software and applications, such as Perl and Python, will need to be manually installed on the target—these are not migrated automatically.

- Register additional components—Specialist DLLs will need to be registered using the regsrvr32.exe tool, and then will need to be included within the Web services extensions if necessary. Also remember to update the COM+/MTS packages if they are used and set any registry values or other settings required by the DLLs.

- Re-create ODBC settings—Use the ODBC Manager to re-create ODBC connections.

- Code conversions—Not all code will run verbatim on the new platform. You will need to test and make appropriate changes before activating the site.

- Local security accounts—These are not migrated, so you will have to re-create them by hand. Also remember to reapply the ACLs for these local users and groups on the target machine.

- FrontPage—The FrontPage administrator account is not created on the target server automatically. You will also need to reset and re-apply FrontPage security settings.

- Windows directory location—You must manually adjust the Windows directory location for components that need it, such as the ScriptMaps and HTTPErrors properties of the Metabase.

- Virtual directory locations—Only the root directory of a Web site is updated; any virtual directory locations that are different will have to be updated.

- Security Certificates—SSL certificates must be migrated and re-imported manually.

- Log files—Log files for individual sites are not migrated; you must do these by hand.

- MIME types—MIME types must be reset or updated by hand.

- IP Address—If you are using multiple IP addresses on a single network interface and are using these additional IP addresses to serve Web sites, you will need to manually add the IP address to the card.

Migrating from Apache to IIS 6

What's New

If you are converting from Apache 1.x under Unix or
Apache 2.0 on more or less any platform, you'll actually
find that there are not as many differences between
Apache and IIS as you might think.

Although Apache is available under Windows, it's more
likely that you will be moving from a Unix platform, and
this adds additional levels of complication. The basic setup
of the two retains some consistency specifics, such as the
way permissions and authentication work and the way in
which external dynamic components integrate with the
server software, and just help to complicate matters even
further.

The execution model now followed by IIS 6 when working
in Worker Application Isolation Mode is very similar to the
'forked' and thread methods used by Apache under most
Unix platforms. Within Apache, individual threads or
duplicate instances of the main Apache server are used to
actually serve the requests of individual clients. Should a
thread or process fail, it's simply recreated to service the
next request.

More critical, though, is the difference between the way
the two systems are administered and the terminology.
Typically, Apache is configured through a text file and
administered, such as you can, through a very simple
application for starting and stopping the entire service. IIS
enables individual sites, and even application pools within
sites, to be controlled individually.

Terminology differences are more difficult to describe without looking at specifics, but one of the most critical to appreciate is the terms used for executable and dynamic components. Within Apache, we are used to CGI scripts handling most dynamic elements, with modules such as mod_perl and mod_php providing an internal solution. Within IIS, we not only have CGI support, but also ISAPI filters—which are a bit like multi-stage CGI scripts.

Administration

With its Unix roots, the majority of administrators reconfigure Apache by directly editing the test file, and then either restarting the Apache process manually or through the `apachectl` command.

Some administrators will use the various Web-based editors, such as Webmin, for administering their site. Webmin is not a complete solution to the hands-on style of the httpd.conf file, but it provides an easier interface for the configuration of some of the core elements.

IIS provides a number of solutions. As well as the familiar command-line and text-based configurations, I can also use Web and GUI-based tools. These are all available locally and remotely.

Starting Up and Shutting Down

Without modifying the configuration file, Apache can only shut down or start up all the sites it has been configured to handle.

Within IIS, I can shut down and start up individual Web sites according to our needs without affecting other sites. To start or stop a particular site, right-click on the site in IIS Manager and select the appropriate option from the pop-up menu.

To start or stop specific sites from the command line, you need to use the `iisweb` tool. For example, to stop a specific site, you would use

```
C:\> iisweb /stop "Default Web Site"
```

To start it up again

```
C:\> iisweb /start "Default Web Site"
```

Note the use of double quotes around the Web site's name—required because the name contains spaces.

Interface-based Administration

The IIS Manager is the normal method of manipulation for IIS. I've already covered many of the facilities, wizards, and tools available in this environment throughout this book. IIS

Manager provides some benefits over the typical text/configuration file interface in that it's often much easier to monitor and modify the configuration, particularly of multiple hosts.

Text-based Administration

If you prefer to administer your Web server by editing a text file, you can edit the IIS Metabase—the equivalent of the Apache httpd.conf file—directly.

▶ For more information on how to edit the Metabase, see Chapter 4, "Management and Monitoring," **p.65**.

Remember that for it to work properly, you must switch on the Enable Direct Metabase Edit property for the server. This will allow you to directly edit the file while IIS is still running. Any edits should automatically be picked up and then reflected within IIS.

Command-line Administration

I've already demonstrated some examples of command-line based administration of a Web site in this chapter. You can, in fact, control most aspects of IIS through a combination of editing the Metabase and using the various command-line tools. See Chapter 4 for more information on the command-line tools and options available.

If you want to be able to perform command-line administration remotely through a Telnet connection, you'll also need to enable the Telnet service. To do this, perform these steps:

1. Open the Services Manager through Start, Administrative Tools, Services.

2. Double-click on the Telnet service to open its property page, as shown in Figure 8.1.

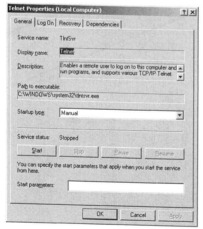

FIGURE 8.1   Setting properties for the Telnet service.

3. Change the Startup type to Automatic so that the service will start automatically when the server is started and then click the Start button to start the service now.

TELNET AND SECURITY

Just as with telnet under Unix, starting up telnet access under Windows also opens up the machine to potential abuse. Make sure that your firewall is configured to block telnet access—except from VPN connections or, at an absolute minimum, from specific IP addresses.

Once started, you'll be able to log in to the server and gain a started Command Prompt, just as if you'd started the Command Prompt application on the local host.

Log Files

In Apache, log files are created as text files usually in the World Wide Web Consortium's (W3C) default format. Various tools are available that can be used to report from and collate the information in these files in to usable reports.

IIS supports standard logging in W3C Extended Log format (the default for new sites) and customized formats. IIS also supports a number of IIS specific formats that include a new binary format in IIS 6. You can also configure IIS to log accesses directly into an ODBC connected database.

NO DEDICATED ERROR LOG

One of the most frequent queries I hear is "Where is my error log?" In IIS, there is unfortunately no provision for creating a separate error log —the errors are placed in the main logging file, just as if you were using the combined log format within Apache. Note that some serious errors are logged by IIS to the Windows Application event log.

Log file properties are set within the WebSite property tab. You can see the configuration, including the available log options, in Figure 8.2.

Logs also have their own set of logging properties. These set facilities automatically create a new log file after a set period (day, hour, file size), as well as the location of the files. The default location is C:\Windows\system32\LogFiles. You can see the property window in Figure 8.3.

You can create customized logs—just as you can in Apache—by clicking the Advanced tab and selecting the specific fields that you want to populate within the log file.

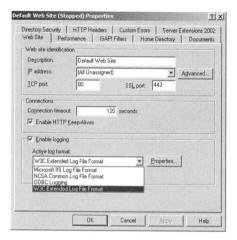

FIGURE 8.2   Setting logging properties.

FIGURE 8.3   Standard logging and rotation properties.

Site Configuration

Apache uses a text file for nearly all aspects of its configuration once installed. The main configuration file is typically called httpd.conf and is either within the Apache installation directory or in the global /etc directory—sometimes within its own /etc/httpd or /etc/apache directory.

Aside from the directory level configuration information, provided by the .htaccess file within each directory, and files imported during startup, the Apache configuration file is the location for everything from default documents and extension/application mappings to the setup of the individual Web sites.

If you are used to this text-based interface for configuration, you are in for your greatest shock with IIS, because the typical administration mode is to use the MMC-based GUI interface. If you use a Web-based interface, such as Webmin, to configure Apache, you can continue to use a Web interface with IIS.

▶ See Chapter 4 for more information on the various methods for administering IIS. Also see the "Administration" section earlier in this chapter (**p.xxx**).

 WEB RESOURCE

For a tutorial on how to translate basic Web site configurations from Apache to IIS, including migrating virtual hosts (the VirtualHost directive), go to the Delta Guide series Web site at www.deltaguideseries.com and enter article ID# **A020901**.

Directory Level Options

The Options directive in Apache Directory directives and .htaccess files is used to enable directory specific options. IIS configures these properties on a Web site or directory basis through the Directory or Home Directory properties for the folder or Web site.

To enable CGI/ISAPI execution in a directory in IIS, equivalent to the ExecCGI option in Apache, follow these steps:

1. Right-click the directory and select Properties.

2. Click the Home Directory or Directory tab.

3. Choose the execute permission for a script by using the pop-up list in Execute Permissions.

4. To enable the execution of specific extensions with specific applications, click Create to create a new application and click Configuration to edit the file extension/application mappings.

▶ See also the information on enabling/configuring Dynamic Solutions in the section "Dynamic Solutions," **p. 155**.

To enable users to browse the directory contents in IIS, equivalent to the Indexes option in Apache, follow these steps:

1. Right-click the directory and select Properties.

2. Click on the Home Directory or Directory tab.

3. Click the Directory Browsing box.

URL Redirection

You can redirect URLs within Apache using the `Redirect` directive to point a folder or location to a different folder on the same Web site or to a different Web site. You can also alias a directory to another location using the `Alias` directive. Both these facilities can be handled within IIS using the URL Redirection system.

To redirect a directory or file within IIS, follow these steps:

1. Right-click the Web site or a folder within the Web site, and then select Open.

2. Right-click the file or directory, and then select Properties.

3. Switch to the Directory panel if redirecting a directory or the File panel if redirecting a file (see Figure 8.4).

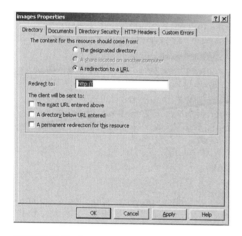

FIGURE 8.4   Setting redirection.

4. Choose A Redirection to a URL.

5. To redirect the file or the entire directory to another URL, click The Exact URL Entered Above and type the full URL to the new site in the Redirect To box.

6. To redirect a directory to another directory below this one—that is, `/projects` to `/sections/departments/projects`—click A Directory Below This One and enter the new directory in the Redirect To box.

7. To mark either redirection type as a permanent redirection, rather than a temporary one, click A Permanent Redirection for This Resource. On some browsers, this will cause bookmarks and other details to be automatically updated.

8. Click OK to save the changes you made.

URL Rewriting

Apache uses a regular expression system to rewrite or redirect URLs to different folders, files, or directories. The same facility is available within IIS by using a combination of wildcards and replacement variables, summarized in Table 8.1.

TABLE 8.1   Special Variables in URL Rewriting

Variable	Description	Example
$S	Passes the last matched element from a URL.	If /scripts is redirected to /newscripts and the original request is for /scripts/program.exe, /program.exe is the suffix. The server automatically performs this suffix substitution; you use the $S variable only in combination with other variables.
$P	Passes the parameters in the original URL.	For example, if the original URL is /scripts/myscript.asp?number=1, the string "number=1" is mapped into the destination URL.
$Q	As $P, but includes leading question mark.	For example, if the original URL is /scripts/myscript.asp?number=1, the string "?number=1" is mapped into the destination URL.
$V	Passes the requested URL, without the server name.	For example, if the original URL is //myserver/scripts/myscript.asp, the string "/scripts/myscript.asp" is mapped into the destination URL.
$0 through $9	Passes the portion of the requested URL that matches the indicated wildcard.	
!	Do not redirect.	Use this variable to prevent redirecting a subdirectory or an individual file in a virtual directory that has been redirected.

You can also use wildcards; those supported by IIS are the * (asterisk) for one or more characters and ? (question mark) for a single character.

You use the redirection facility discussed in redirection to activate the rewriting; the Redirect to box holding the source and the destination URL, separated by a semicolon.

For example, to redirect all the files ending in .html to the file default.html, follow these steps:

1. Right-click on the folder you want to use as the base for rewriting, and then select Properties.

2. Switch to the Directory panel.

3. Choose A Redirection to a URL.

4. Click The Exact URL Entered Above.

5. Type ***.html;default.html** in the Redirect To box.

6. Click OK to accept the changes.

To redirect the query for a script to an alternative script—that is, myscript.asp?number=1 to the script newscript?number=1—follow these steps:

1. Right-click on the original script, and then select Properties.

2. Switch to the File panel.

3. Choose A Redirection to a URL.

4. Click The Exact URL Entered Above.

5. Type **newscript.asp$Q** in the Redirect To box.

6. Click OK to accept the changes.

Setting Default Documents

Within Apache, you can control which document is served to a client if a specific document in a directory is not requested. You do this using the DirectoryIndex directive:

```
DirectoryIndex index.cgi index.shtml index.html
```

The order of the documents listed is important because it adjusts the priority. In the preceding example, if both the index.cgi and index.shtml documents exist in a directory, index.cgi will be executed and returned to the client.

In IIS, we can achieve the same result by modifying the Documents setting for a directory. Within Apache, you can also set an alternative default document list for a specific directory using the DirectoryIndex directive within a Directory directive in the main configuration file or an .htaccess file.

IIS supports both Web site and directory level configuration. To set the default documents and their priority in IIS for an entire Web site or a specific directory, follow these steps:

1. Right-click the Web site or directory in the IIS Manager and select Properties.

2. Click the Documents tab.

3. Check the Enable Default Documents box to enable default documents.

4. Click Add to add the name of a file or script to be used as a default document.

5. Use the Move Up and Move Down buttons to change the priority of the listed files; those at the top will be selected first (if they exist).

Note that the changes you make become available immediately; you do not need to restart IIS to adjust these settings.

As with Apache, if you want the default document list to include a script, you must have created an association between the file's extension and the application or library used to parse and evaluate the document.

Setting Error Documents

Error documents within Apache are configured through the ErrorDocument directive. In IIS, they are configured on a directory or Web site basis through the corresponding properties page and the Custom Errors tab.

You have three options: You can either return a standard, IIS formatted message; you can redirect the error to an HTML document; or you can redirect the user to an alternative URL.

To change the configuration, follow these steps:

1. Create a file that contains your custom error message and place it in a folder or within your Web site's directory.

2. In the IIS Manager snap-in, select the Web site, virtual folder, folder, or file in which you want to customize HTTP error messages, and click Properties.

3. On the Custom Errors property sheet, select the HTTP error message that you want to change and click Edit Properties.

4. In the Message Type box, select Default for the default message, File to redirect to a fixed file, or URL to redirect to a URL.

5. If redirecting to a file, type the path and filename that points to your customized error message, or use the Browse button to locate the file on your computer's hard disk. If using a URL, type the URL into the box provided. Click OK.

ERROR REDIRECTION
You can only redirect major errors (that is, 400, 404, and so on) to a URL. IIS specific sub-errors and messages can only be sourced from a file or can only use the default IIS text.

REDIRECTING ERRORS
If you redirect an error to an ASP page, the error number and original URL of the error are supplied to the ASP page as arguments.

FTP Services

Although not an Apache service, FTP is often used in combination with Apache-based installations when files need to be downloaded or where two-way communication with a client is required and WebDAV or multipart HTTP requests are not in use.

▶ One of the common reasons to use FTP for file downloads is that the number of concurrent users can be very tightly controlled. You can achieve this level of control through HTTP services by using the queue length and worker process tuning facilities provided by IIS 6. See Chapter 2, "Architecture and Execution," **p. 15**, for more information.

FTP sites are created within IIS in much the same way as Web sites—you right-click on the server in the IIS manager and create an FTP site through a wizard.

Previously, IIS 5 and lower provided a simple FTP service. Although it provided FTP services, upload/download facilities, and authenticated logins, all authenticated users were placed in to the same directory once they had connected to the server. This meant that although you could restrict access to those users with passwords, you couldn't then restrict them from accessing or overwriting files placed in the same directory by other authenticated users.

IIS 6 improves on that by providing three different types of user isolation when you are creating the FTP site (description in parentheses are the corresponding options from within the wizard):

- **No Isolation (Do Not Isolate Users)**—This is identical to previous versions of IIS— with all authenticated users being placed within the same directory when they log in.

- **Isolation (Isolate Users)**—This is identical to the Unix style FTP service—authenticated users are placed into a corresponding user directory that is isolated from all other users. The user is able to control all aspects of his directory, provided that you've granted him access, but he won't be able to affect other user's files.

- **Isolation Through Active Directory (Isolate Users Using Active Directory)**— This authenticates users against AD and then transparently maps their FTP root directory into the home directory as configured in AD.

Security Conversions

There are two aspects to the security of Web sites—the physical access to the files and scripts being accessed by clients and the authentication of those clients to access the information in the first place.

In this section, I'll have a look at two specific areas: the basic permissions systems and how to translate permissions from the Unix and Apache sides over to the Windows and IIS equivalents.

Understanding NTFS/IIS Security

Apache under Unix uses both the underlying permissions on the file system and directory level settings within the Apache configuration to determine which files are served to a particular client. Authentication methods vary, but the standard solutions include basic and digest authentication and extensions provide access to external databases and sources such as LDAP for identification.

Often this difference between the systems can make it difficult to identify and repair security/access problems because the three systems are separate. The underlying filesystem bears no relation to the options within Apache, and the authentication system is not related to the same system used for the underlying filesystem.

IIS also uses a two-tier security system for controlling access to the underlying files using both the NTFS and IIS permissions to determine a user's access to the files in a given folder. However, because of the underlying filesystem (typically NTFS), IIS and the authentication system use the same Active Directory or local (server specific) authentication database for identifying users.

IIS also uses different methods for identifying and handling executable components (scripts, CGI, and so on) and more simplistic elements, such as directory browsing.

All these differences make migrating the settings from Apache to IIS more difficult. To add to the complication, the permissions on files in both the filesystem and IIS are also different. In most editions of Unix, the only system available for controlling access to the files is the user/group/other and read/write/execute model, where you can grant access to files and folders based on the combination of the preceding settings.

Within Windows and IIS, you can specify seven basic permissions, including read, write, and execute, on any user and group in any combination. This is better known as the Access Control List (ACL) method and is supported by some Unix flavors (for example, HP-UX) and some filesystem types, such as Andrew Filesystem (AFS). You can see an example of the access permissions window in Figure 8.5.

For example, under Unix you might have a file owned by wwwuser, group ownership is set to wwwgroup with permissions or rw-rw-r--, which provides read/write access to wwwuser and members of the wwwgroup, but with read-only access for everybody else. If I wanted to provide read/write access to another user, I'd have to add him to the group, which could then present problems because he could now be part of a group that also grants him access to other items.

Within Windows and NTFS, I could specifically provide read/write access to both the wwwuser and wwwgroup and read-only access to the Everyone special group, identical to the basic Unix permissions. If I wanted to provide additional access to another user, I would just add him to the access control list. His ability to access the file wouldn't provide him with any additional access or compromise the security of other objects.

FIGURE 8.5 Access control list settings in Windows.

MIGRATING ACLS

In most situations, you won't need to migrate access control lists from one platform to another, or indeed use the ACL features when migrating from a standard Unix permissions system, but you should be aware that such a system exists so that you can remove access from users and groups on default.

Translating Unix Permissions to NTFS

Most Unix platforms use a simple user/group/other and read/write/execute combination for setting permissions for a given file or directory. For example, it's possible to set a file as readable by everybody, but writable only by the user and group owner. There are also some specific behaviors—for example, only directories with execute permissions can have their directory contents (list of files/directories) accessed. Finally, the execute permission bit is used on files to identify those that can be executed. If the file is recognized as a binary file, it is executed as a native binary. If it's a text file, the first line is examined to check which application should be used to execute the file.

Windows uses a slightly different model, although the basics remain the same. Files and directories can have read and write permissions, but these are granted explicitly to individual users or groups of users, rather than the owner, group owner, or everybody else. You can also select whether to explicitly allow or deny this ability to this user or group. This model is similar to the Access Control List model used by some Unix variants. There are also specific permissions for listing directory content. There are no execute permissions on files. Windows uses the file extension to determine whether a file is executable, including script files.

The basic rules for translating these settings are as follows:

- Read permission on a directory in Unix is the same as Read permission in Windows.

- Write permission on a directory in Unix is the same as Write permission in Windows.

- Read and Execute permissions on a file in Unix are the same as Read and Execute permission in Windows.

- Write permission on a file in Unix is the same as Modify permission in Windows.

- Execute permission on a directory in Unix is the same as List Folder Contents permission in Windows.

- Read, Write, Execute permissions on a file or directory in Unix is the same as Full Control permission in Windows.

To set the permissions for a file or directory within Windows, follow these steps:

1. Use Explorer to locate the file or directory that you want to adjust permissions for.

2. Right-click on the directory and select Properties.

3. Click Security to change to the security panel.

4. To add a new access control setting to the directory, click Add. You will be asked to select the Users, Computers, or Groups that this access control setting will be applied to. Select the entries and click Add. Click OK when you have made your selection.

5. To remove an access control setting, click Remove.

6. To edit the permissions for any group, select the user or group and then use the corresponding check boxes in the Permissions panel.

7. Click OK to accept the settings. Click Cancel to cancel any changes you have made. Click Apply to apply the changes without closing the properties window.

Translating Apache Permissions to IIS

Within Apache, it is the underlying permissions of the Unix filesystem and the owner/group that the Apache server is being executed under that affect which objects can be accessed and which scripts can be executed.

Within Windows, IIS effectively executes as the administrator with potential access to any file within the tree of the home directory for a configured Web site. The underlying Windows permissions for a directory or file are ignored. Instead, a separate mechanism within IIS allows you to control and limit the types of access for a given object to clients.

The Read permission in IIS is directly analogous to the Read permission bit for file within Apache/Unix. The Write permission in IIS is used only when using ASP scripts or WebDAV to provide update facilities for a file, and is therefore analogous to the write permission in Apache/Unix for WebDAV only.

Execute permissions in Unix, combined with the AddHandler directive, indicate to Apache that a particular file is a script and should be executed rather than returned as a raw file. In IIS, execute permissions are granted on a Web site or directory basis only—individual files cannot be enabled or disabled as scripts in this way. However, the extension/handler combination does apply. You grant execute permissions for a directory, and then associate an extension with a specific scripting engine.

This has limitations because you cannot use a blanket .cgi extension and rely on the Unix header line to select the corresponding scripting language, which might cause problems during migration. Instead, you must, for example, associate the .pl extension for Perl scripts and .py extension for Python scripts.

Object-Level Security

Security within IIS is configurable on an object-by-object basis—that is, per file, as well as per directory and Web site.

To set the permissions for an object within IIS, follow these steps:

1. Right-click on the object and select Properties.

2. If setting the permissions for a Web site's home directory, select the Home Directory panel.

3. If setting the permissions for a directory within a Web site, select the Directory panel.

4. If setting the permissions for a file or script within a directory, select the File panel.

5. Click the corresponding permissions that you want to enable for the object concerned.

6. To enable script processing for a website or directory, select Scripts Only from the Execute permissions list. To disable script processing, select None.

7. Click OK to accept the Web site properties.

▶ For more information on how the different permissions work and how they relate to their Apache/Unix equivalents, see "Translating Unix Permissions to NTFS," (**p.149**) and "Translating Apache Permissions to IIS," (**p.150**), earlier in this chapter.

Restricting by IP Address or Domain Name

Apache uses the Allow and Deny directives to determine which sites can and can't access a particular Web site or directory. The system provides discretionary access control—you must either deny all sites and provide a specific list of sites or IP addresses that can access a directory, or you allow all sites and deny only those you do not want to have access.

For example,

```
Deny from all
Allow from .domain.com
```

would deny all clients access unless they were recognized as part of the domain.com domain.

The IIS system works in exactly the same way. All clients are specifically denied or granted access, except for those listed.

To define the access control for a given directory or site, follow these steps:

1. If you want to limit access for the entire site, select the Web site from the list of different served sites in the panel on the left. If you only want to limit access for a specific directory, choose the directory you want to control.

2. Right-click on the Web site or directory and select Properties.

3. Select the Directory Security panel.

4. If you want to limit access to a specific set of sites but deny it to all others, select Denied Access.

5. If you want to allow all clients by default but exclude a specific list of clients, select Granted Access.

6. To update the list of hosts or domains in the Except list, click Add.

7. To add a single computer to the list, click Single computer. Enter the IP address into the box and click OK.

8. To add a range of computers within a specific address range, click Group of Computers. Enter the IP address for the network and the subnet mask for the desired network range, and then click OK.

9. To add computers by their identified domain name, click Domain name. Enter the domain name.

10. Click Properties to open the Extended Properties dialog box. Enter the domain name and click OK.

11. Click OK to accept the security settings.

12. Click OK to close the Properties dialog box.

DOMAIN NAME RESTRICTIONS = OVERHEAD
Using domain name restrictions puts a heavy load on the server because it has to perform a reverse DNS lookup for each request to check the host's registered domain name. Try to use an IP address or network range where possible.

Authentication

If you are using Apache or httpd password files under Apache/Unix or are using the Unix authentication system (/etc/passwd), the user/group information is stored within a simple text file. All users under Windows must be created within the Windows Server 2003 directory, either local on the machine or as part of Active Directory, just as if they were standard users.

TRANSFERRING PASSWORDS
Doing this by hand would be time-consuming. A tool is in the Windows 2000 Resource Kit called AddUsers that will translate slightly modified Unix passwd and group files and transfer them to Active Directory. The same tool should be available for Windows Server 2003, although I haven't been able to confirm this. You can check Microsoft Knowledge Base Article #324222 for more information on this tool. Alternatively, use the Apache Migration Tool from the IIS 6 Resource Kit.

If you have users stored in NIS/NIS+ and you need to migrate them, you must use Services for Unix to perform the migration.

When your users are within the Windows authentication database, you can set authentication for a Web site or folder using the IIS MMC snap-in.

▶ You need to refer to the instructions and guidance in Chapter 3, "Security," (**p.39**), for more information on the authentication options within IIS 6.

Typically the following rules apply when migrating the settings:

- Standard (non-authenticated) access within Apache is equivalent to Anonymous access within IIS 6.

- Standard and digest authentication within Apache are equivalent to Basic authentication within IIS 6.

- Integrated Windows authentication enables a user logged in with an authenticated account on a Windows client into the site without a password prompt, providing that his account is within the authentication parameters (that is, member of an appropriate account).

Migrating .htaccess Data

Directory level configuration data, such as that supplied through an .htaccess file, is probably the hardest element to reproduce effectively within IIS.

Although IIS includes directory level configuration—as I've already demonstrated—it's not something that is typically available to end users, only administrators.

Some tricks, however, can be applied at a user level. For example, if the user has the ability to control permissions on the folder in which the files for his Web site or Web site directory are located, he can modify the properties. However, setting authentication and other options will have to be handled by an administrator.

Some additional options are often configured through .htaccess, even if they can't be user defined, and are discussed in the sections that follow.

Setting Directory Options

The basic options for a given directory that are normally set by the Apache Options directive are configured in a number of different places.

▶ See "Directory Level Options," **p. 142**, for more information.

Restricting Access by IP Address

The .htaccess file uses the Order, Allow, and Deny directives to limit access by IP address or domain name. Unfortunately, it is not possible to control this at a user level. To limit by IP address or domain name in IIS, follow the instructions given earlier.

▶ See "Restricting by IP Address or Domain Name," **p. 151**

Setting Authentication

To set the authentication options for a directory or file, you must first migrate your user's and group's information to your Windows Server 2003 host. Then follow the instructions given earlier in this chapter. Unfortunately, it is not possible to control this at a user level.

▶ See "Authentication," **p. 153**, for more information.

Redirecting URLs

The .htaccess file uses the Redirect directive to redirect a file or directory to another URL. For example,

```
Redirect /oldfile.html http://www.domain.com/newdir/newfile.html
```

I've already described some methods for redirecting requests. For a user-defined solution, you can create a file called Default.asp in the directory where you want to redirect. Then use the Response.Redirect statement within ASP to redirect a request for a particular element. For example, we could rewrite the previous as

```
Response.Redirect /oldfile.html http://www.domain.com/newdir/newfile.html
```

You can repeat this as many times as you like to redirect different URLs.

Dynamic Solutions

Unless you have a very simple Web site, chances are that you will have some dynamic elements to your Web site. Server Side Includes are a simple way to introduce regularly occurring elements and even dynamic elements into your Web pages.

Irrespective of the development language you have used in the past and how compatible it is across platforms, you should expect to have to make at least a few changes when migrating applications from Unix to Windows.

Even if you've used the built-in tools that manage file naming and location issues or the generic network tools, you might still need to make allowances. Also, keep in mind that many extensions beyond the core language will require recompilation or resourcing to work within the Windows environment. A good example here is the DBI extensions used for connecting to databases in Perl.

Remember that if you are using CGI or ISAPI methods, you will need to enable them through the Web Service Extension manager within the IIS MMC snap-in. You can see an example of the manager in Figure 8.6.

Once you've added a particular ISAPI filter, you configure the extensions that work with individual filters—equivalent to the Apache AddHandler directive—through the Directory or Home Directory properties page for a directory or Web site. You can see the page in Figure 8.7.

First, set the Execute permissions to scripts only. Then click the Configuration button to get the mappings window shown in Figure 8.8. This enables you to associate a given file extension with one of the registered ISAPI filters. You can see from the figure, for example, that .pl uses Perl in CGI mode and .plx uses Perl in ISAPI mode.

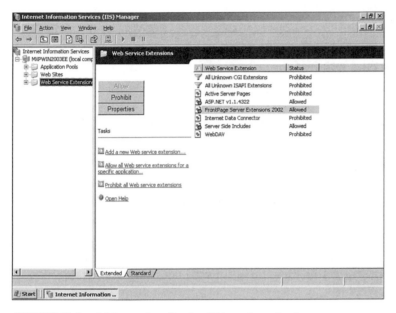

FIGURE 8.6   Adding and configuring Web service extensions.

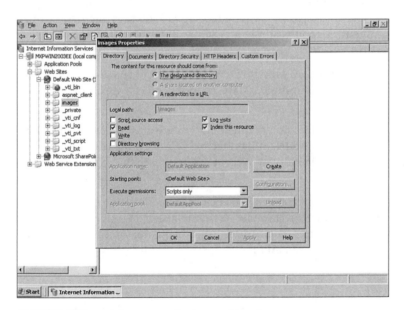

FIGURE 8.7   Configuring applications and handlers.

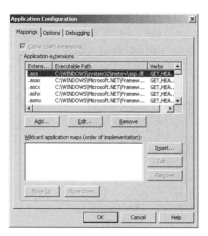

FIGURE 8.8 Associating extensions with ISAPI filters.

Server Side Includes

If all you need is some basic template building and importing of different elements into a page, the obvious choice is usually *Server Side Includes (SSI)*. SSI is processed directly by Apache and is therefore a much more efficient model than using Perl or Python in CGI mode (that is, without the benefit of mod_perl).

You can enable server side includes using the server extensions manager within the IIS MMC snap-in.

 SERVER-SIDE INCLUDES

Remember that SSIs are one way that hackers attempt to attack some Web sites, which is why IIS disables them in a default installation. You will need to specifically enable SSIs in Add/Remove Windows Components before they will be available to you.

Perl

Perl is available on the Windows platform in both original and ActivePerl editions. The ActivePerl Edition, from ActiveState Corporation, includes extensions that enable it to work as an ISAPI filter. The standard installer will correctly install and configure your IIS installation to execute Perl scripts just as if they were CGI scripts under Apache/Unix.

In most instances, the ActivePerl route is the easiest one to take. You should be able to transfer your existing scripts—and any modules and other elements that the scripts need—to your new IIS host, and they should continue to execute normally.

ActivePerl version numbers use the same version numbering system as the main Perl distribution. In addition, ActivePerl gives a 'build' number that indicates the specific build (incorporating new features, enhancements, and bug fixes). For example, the full ActivePerl distribution can be referred to as ActivePerl 5.6.1, Build 631. You should always choose the latest 'stable' build of the ActivePerl distribution.

If you want a faster solution, you can essentially embed the Perl interpreter into IIS using PerlEx, which is also from ActiveState. The embedding provided by PerlEx is similar to the functionality provided by mod_perl, although unlike mod_perl, it's limited to execution of Perl scripts, not a general-purpose extension for using Perl within Apache.

PERL AND IIS 6 WORKER PROCESS ISOLATION
At the time of writing, support for PerlEx in IIS 6 in Worker Process Isolation Mode was uncertain—although it appears to work correctly when used in IIS 5 Isolation Mode.

For more extensive installations in which you want you take full advantage of the Windows platform, you might want to consider PerlASPX, again from ActiveState. PerlASPX is a Perl interpreter built on top of the .NET Framework that enables you to use .NET technologies from within a Perl script. As an ASP.NET service, it offers the best of both worlds—compatibility with your existing Perl applications combined with the capability to interface to the newer features supported by .NET.

For the development environment, you might want to consider VisualPerl, which is an extension to the Visual Studio.NET development environment customized for developing Perl applications. You get the same benefits as other target languages—inline debugger, customized editors, class browsing, and source code control.

Python

Python is also available in a Windows version, and fewer compatibility issues exist when migrating from one platform to another—provided that you've used the generic underlying modules for file naming, network connections, threads, and so on.

ActiveState also provides versions of Python for Windows in the form of ActivePython and a Visual Studio.NET component in the form of VisualPython.

You can obtain the ActivePython software—a special version of the Python language interpreter designed to work under Windows and with additional Windows specific extensions—by downloading the ActivePython installer from the ActiveState Web site.

ActivePython version numbers use the same version numbering system of the main Python distribution. In addition, ActivePython gives a 'build' number, which indicates the specific build (incorporating new features, enhancements, and bug fixes). For example, the full ActivePython distribution can be referred to as ActivePython 2.2.0, Build 221. You should always choose the latest 'stable' build of the ActivePython distribution.

PHP

PHP is also a cross-platform capable Web programming language. An installer is available that includes ISAPI support for the IIS Web serving platform. As with Perl and Python applications, the majority should migrate to Windows/IIS without any modifications.

PHP is available in two different distributions:

- A ZIP package, which includes support for CGI PHP scripts and server API extensions for the ISAPI system supported by IIS. This package also comes with built-in support for interfacing to the MySQL database and a complete suite of additional extensions.

- An installer package, which includes support for CGI based PHP scripts and MySQL. Support for ISAPI is not included, and neither are additional external extensions. However, the installation is much more straightforward.

USING ZIP

I recommend the ZIP because you get the ISAPI extension, although the installation is slightly more complex.

To install from the ZIP package, follow these basic steps:

1. Extract the ZIP package using WinZip or the built-in Zip extraction tool.

2. Copy the directory extracted to a suitable location. The recommended location is C:\PHP.

3. Follow the instructions in the install.txt document that comes with the package. Be careful because some of the steps require you to edit the registry directly.

MySQL

Dynamic sites often take advantage of some sort of database, and the most popular solution outside of the commercial solutions, such as DB2 or Oracle, is MySQL. MySQL is also available for Windows and can be used in combination with Perl, Python, and other scripting languages and even ASP/ASP.NET as a SQL solution.

To install MySQL under Windows, follow these steps:

1. Unpack the MySQL distribution using WinZip or the built-in compressed folders tool.

2. Change to the MySQL directory, and double-click Setup to start the MySQL installer.

3. Click Next to continue the installation.

4. Read the installation notes, and click Next to confirm that you are happy with the default settings.

5. Check the installation directory. The default location is C:\MySQL. If you change this location, you will need to modify the MySQL configuration file, as mentioned in the previous release notes screen. Click Browse to choose a different install directory. Click Next to continue installation.

6. Choose the type of installation. The Typical installation includes all the elements that you should need to run MySQL. A Compact installation installs only the minimum amount required to use MySQL. Custom allows you to select which elements to install. Click Next to continue the installation.

7. If you selected the Custom installation setting, you will be asked to select which elements of MySQL you want to install. Check the items you want to include in your installation. Click Next to continue the installation.

8. The installation will now start. Once the files have been installed, click Finish to terminate the installer.

You will need to build the initial databases used to hold the grant and security information before you can start using the MySQL database. Follow the instructions given in the MySQL documentation, which you can find in the Docs directory of the installation directory.

 PERL, PYTHON, MYSQL, AND MORE

Why bother installing these non-Microsoft technologies? They're very popular in Apache installations, and if you're migrating to IIS, things will be much smoother if you don't have to rewrite the Web pages and redesign the database at the same time.

ASP/ASP.NET

Retooling all of your software for ASP/ASP.NET is not a simple undertaking and shouldn't be considered lightly. Most solutions already mentioned—Perl, Python, and PHP, in particular—should be relatively trouble free and are frequently used as first-time solutions under IIS.

Shellscript

Shellscript is not a standard CGI environment for developing dynamic Web sites, but it is used by some environments either as a CGI scripting language or as a utility language used to batch process logs, requests, or other information for processing elsewhere.

Native support doesn't exist for any of the Unix Shellscript environments within Windows, but some solutions are available. The most obvious of these is Microsoft's own Services for Unix (SFU) and Cygwin, a Unix/Linux like environment for Windows based on the GNU toolset.

SFU provides a combination of support environments for certain Unix stalwarts, shellscripts included, as well as compatibility interfaces and services for Unix hosts, such as NFS client/server support and an NIS-compatible interface to Active Directory. You can use the Shellscript facilities of SFU and Cygwin to execute shellscripts just as you would execute them on a Unix host.

However, neither tool should be seen as a long term solution to the problems of running shellscripts. If you rely heavily on shellscripts for CGI solutions, you should migrate them as quickly as possible. Move them to a cross-platform solution, which will retain compatibility with your Unix installation, especially useful during a migration. Alternatively, if you do not need to retain compatibility, instead migrate them to ASP/ASP.NET.

If they are utility scripts, move them to batch files if you can—the closest Windows equivalent to Shellscript—or, better still, move them to Visual Basic.

Java

Java code should run fine under Windows without modification. If you are using Java Server Pages (JSP) or servlets, you will need to install a JSP/Servlet runner application. The most obvious of these should actually be familiar to you if you use Apache under Unix. It's Tomcat, another of the Apache Software Foundation's projects.

In many ways, getting Tomcat working under IIS is no different than getting Tomcat working under Unix. Installation requires a few careful steps:

1. Download and install the Sun Win32 Java Development Kit (JDK); you can download it from `http://java.sun.com`. Using version 1.4.1, this should install Java in to C:\j2sdk1.4.1_01 by default.

2. Download and install the Tomcat installer package (from `http://jakarta.apache.org`). When asked to select installation options, make sure that you check the NT Service box. Make a note of the installation directory—with Tomcat 4.1.x, it should be something like C:\Program Files\Apache Group\Tomcat 4.1.

3. Right click My Computer, Properties, choose the Advanced panel, and then click Environmental Variables. Set TOMCAT_HOME to the location of the Tomcat installation directory and JAVA_HOME to the location of the JDK. Modify PATH so that the first entry is the bin directory within the JDK installation directory.

If you now open a browser to your server on port 8080—that is, `http://localhost:8080/` from the server itself—you should get the Tomcat default homepage.

IIS 6 AND TOMCAT

There are ways in which you can connect Tomcat and IIS through an ISAPI redirector, but support for this under IIS 6 is uncertain at the time of writing. Check the Jakarta Tomcat project homepage (`http://Jakarta.apache.org`) for the most up-to-date information.

Compiled Code

All compiled code—irrespective of the source language—will need to be recompiled under Windows. Visual Studio.NET incorporates a C/C++ compiler if you need one and also provides a rich environment for developing Windows and .NET specific applications and tools.

If you are using compiled applications, you might want to consider retooling the project with ASP/ASP.NET.

Deployment Options

Choosing a method for actually deploying Your Apache to IIS migration is more difficult. The obvious steps to the migration are as follows:

1. Migrate the basic configuration.

2. Migrate the static Web files (HTML, graphics).

3. Migrate the applications and dynamic components.

4. Migrate authentication/security.

 WEB RESOURCE

For a tutorial on how to migrate files from Unix to Windows and IIS, go to the Delta Guide series Web site at www.deltaguideseries.com and enter article ID# **A020902**

After the actual physical migration has completed, you then need to test your installation. Typically, I recommend a period of at least one month testing the new platform followed by a month testing the system in tandem with your existing installation to iron out bugs. For a major Web site, I'd increase those figures to three and three.

During the testing, test the existing site and then test the new site, checking both for missing links and bad components and performance. You should then be able to make suitable comparisons for the new system.

If you want to ease the migration process, two tools can help you. The first is the Apache Migration Tool that comes with the IIS 6 Resource Kit; the second is Services For Unix, which can help to migrate user and authentication information, as well as the data and files.

I've given a brief overview of the main components and facilities of the two systems here.

Apache Migration Tool

The IIS 6 Resource Kit comes with a migration tool, which can perform many of the main functions of a migration for you, including copying the source files, copying certain aspects of the configuration and security, and modifying source HTML to take into account location/server changes.

The migration tool will migrate Linux (Red Hat, Mandrake, and SuSE varieties are the only ones recommended) running Apache 1.3.x only. You can perform the migration either directly from a Windows Server 2003 host, from the Linux host, or through an intermediate host that marshals information from the source to the destination.

The migration should work relatively painlessly with most of the directives and information being transferred without intervention. However, it's not perfect. It doesn't transfer all the directives from Apache—mostly because of differences in the way the two systems operate—and it's translation of files is limited to any name or location changes. Issues with scripts or dynamic elements are not handled, and even if your site is entirely composed of static HTML and graphics, there is no guarantee the site will transfer without problems.

Table 8.2 contains a list of the Apache directives that are translated and migrated to IIS during the process.

TABLE 8.2   Directives Migrated by the IIS 6 Resource Kit Apache Migration Tool

Directive	Notes (where applicable)
AddEncoding/AddType	Migrates the settings to the MIME Types settings within IIS 6.
Alias	Creates a virtual directory object.
AuthGroupFile	Groups in the file are migrated to the local authentication system for the server (not AD).
AuthName	Adjusts the Realm property for the corresponding directory in the authentication settings.
AuthType	Applies the equivalent authorization type to the directory.
AuthUserFile	Users in the file are migrated to the local authentication system for the server (not AD).
BindAddress	
DefaultType	
<Directory>, <DirectoryMatch>	Migrated, but ExpiresDefault and IdentityCheck do not have equivalents in IIS.
DirectoryIndex	
DocumentRoot	
ErrorDocument	
ErrorLog	Not migrated, but errors in IIS are recorded in the main logs.
ExpiresActive	Sets the Enable content expiration property.
ExpiresDefault	There is no equivalent in IIS 6, so instead the Expire immediately property is enabled.

TABLE 8.2 Continued

Directive	Notes (where applicable)
<Files>	All tags except ExpiresDefault and IdentityCheck are migrated.
<FilesMatch>	All tags except ExpiresDefault and IdentityCheck are migrated.
Header	
HostnameLookups	Only sets hostname lookups on or off—the *double* property in Apache is not migrated.
IdentityCheck	Enables Extended logging properties for the log for a Web site.
KeepAlive	Sets the Enable HTTP Keep Alives property.
KeepAliveTimeout	Migrated to the Connection timeout property.
Listen	
ListenBacklog	
MaxClients	Migrated to the Connections limited to property for the site.
NameVirtualHost	
Options	Only the ExecCGI and Indexes options are migrated. Other options to this directive are not supported or have no direct equivalent in IIS 6.
Port	Only migrates ports with numbers less than 65,535.
ResourceConfig	File referenced by this directive is parsed for context purposes.
ScriptAlias	
ServerAlias	Sets the host header information.
ServerName	Sets the name as it appears within IIS manager.
ServerRoot	
SSLEngine	The information is not migrated, but the migration tool prompts for the information.
TypesConfig	
UserDir	User directories are migrated to corresponding virtual directories within the default Web space.
<VirtualHost>	

▶ If your site is in any way more complex than basic HTML, I'd recommend that you migrate the system using a more pragmatic step-by-step process that migrates individual components or areas of the sites and tests them thoroughly. See "Deployment Options," (**p. 162**) in this chapter for more information.

Services for Unix 3.0

Services for Unix (SFU) is a suite of utilities that allow you to share information and resources between Unix and Windows computers. The main features of SFU of interest during a migration from Apache to IIS are summarized in Table 8.3.

TABLE 8.3 SFU Features

Feature	Description
Unix environment	Enables you to execute Unix scripts and recompile and deploy Unix applications using standard Unix applications, including make, rcs, yacc, lex, cc, c89, nm, strip, gdb, as well as the gcc, g++, and g77 compilers. You also have access to Unix tools such as awk, grep, sed, tr, cut, tar, cpio.
Script Environment	Executes Perl, Korn, and C shell scripts within Windows.
Security Integration	Enables you to communicate and authenticate with NIS servers.
NFS Client/Server	You can now share Windows directories through NFS and also access NFS resources. This makes exchanging files between Unix and Windows environments much easier.

Scalability and Reliability

Clustering Solutions

In Windows Server 2003, there are two clustering solutions, Network Load Balancing (NLB) and Cluster Service. Both systems were available in Windows, but they have been updated in Windows Server 2003. Although both are classed as cluster solutions, they work in different ways and have different advantages and potential uses:

> **Cluster Service** can be used to provide machine-level backup to a system in the event of failure. Typically, it's used within datacenters and enterprise server configurations where you need 100% availability. Clusters can be configured in a number of different ways, but really with one goal in mind—for one machine to take over the responsibilities of another in case it fails.

> **Network Load Balancing** is a software only solution for distributing requests over a number of servers within an NLB cluster. This provides basic failover support by redirecting a request only to a currently active machine and also load balancing by spreading the requests among the machines to make the best of the overall horsepower.

A third technology exists that can also be added to Windows Server 2003 through Microsoft Application Server 2000, which is called Component Load Balancing (CLB). Unlike the other technologies that provide support for clusters irrespective of the specific applications you might be supporting, CLB works at the application level.

Using CLB, individual Common Object Model+ (COM+) components reside on a number of separate servers within a COM+ cluster. This enables you to distribute the workload of an application across multiple servers running a single business application. CLB automatically routes calls to individual COM+ components within the COM+ cluster. It can also be used with a combination of NLB and Cluster Service to provide an additional tier of load balancing within a large Web farm. Refer to the documentation on Microsoft's site for more information on Application Server 2000.

Service Compatibility

Table A.1 shows the cluster services supported by the different operating systems. Note that with Windows Server 2003, there is not a huge amount of disparity between the versions. If you need true clustering services, you need Enterprise or Datacenter Editions, whereas NLB is supported by all versions.

TABLE A.1   Clustering Support in Windows Server 2003 Editions

Edition	NLB	Cluster Nodes
Standard Edition	Y	Not Supported
Enterprise Edition	Y	8
Datacenter Edition	Y	8
Web Edition	Y	Not Supported

This is a marked change over Windows 2000 and Windows NT. Previously, you required the Advanced (now Enterprise) Edition of Windows 2000 to gain NLB. This change again shows that Microsoft is responding to the market demands of lower-level installation and server farms, where NLB would be useful, but the additional features of the Enterprise Edition would be wasted.

Not all services within Windows Server 2003 can be clustered, and in many cases it doesn't make sense for some elements to be supported by the cluster services. For example, remote access is not a critical service, so providing fail-over support is not required. For load distribution, generally the number of physical modems connected to a server will be the limiting factor.

Instead, cluster services concentrate on two main areas:

- Internal services, such as distributed file systems, DHCP, and WINS
- Public services, such as IIS and message queuing

In addition, the clustering types supported by each service are dependent on how the individual service is normally used. For example, with IIS it makes sense to support the cluster service, to provide resiliency, and to provide NLB for request distribution. File services, however, are only supported by the cluster service because there is no way to reliably exchange information about open files between two machines, even if the files are on a shared device.

For a full list of the services that can be clustered, see Table A.2.

TABLE A.2 Services Supported by Clustering Services

Service	NLB	Clustering
Internet Information Service	Yes	Yes
DHCP Service	No	Yes
Distributed File Service Roots	No	Yes
Distributed Transaction Coordinator	No	Yes
File Shares	No	Yes
Message Queuing	No	Yes
Printer Spools	See following note	Yes
Volume Shadow Copy Service Tasks	No	Yes
WINS Service	No	Yes

LOAD BALANCED PRINTERS
You can, technically, cluster print spools by having two servers that both print to the same network attached print device. In practice of course, you've still only got one device actually handling the printing, so the benefits are never really fully realized.

 CLUSTERING IIS?
Although IIS is supported in clustering, there are few instances when it makes sense to do so. It makes more sense to use multiple IIS servers and NLB—you'll get both redundancy and load balancing.

Network Load Balancing

Network Load Balancing provides both failover and load balancing for IIS. The system works through a standard network connection on each machine. Each member of the cluster is configured to use one or more shared IP addresses, in addition to its personal IP address. This means that all members of the cluster receive the request from a client, but only one member responds.

The decision for which machine should respond is based on a set of internal rules and customizable affinity rules. All members of the cluster exchange system load information, which is used by the NLB system to choose the member to process the request.

Failover support is provided by NLB through this exchange of information. Any members that have not communicated their status are removed from the equation.

The primary improvement in Windows Server 2003 for Network Load Balancing is the move to a single administration application, called the NLB Manager. This greatly simplifies the setup of an NLB cluster. Unlike Windows 2000, you no longer have to set up each machine individually.

Instead, you create the NLB cluster on one machine. Individual members of the cluster can be added from within NLB Manager without the need to visit each machine.

The NLB Manager handles all aspects of the configuration for all members within the cluster, automatically propagating changes to each member. Furthermore, NLB Manager enables you to manage multiple clusters simply by connecting to an existing cluster.

You can see the NLB Manager in action, showing the status of a newly created cluster, in Figure A.1.

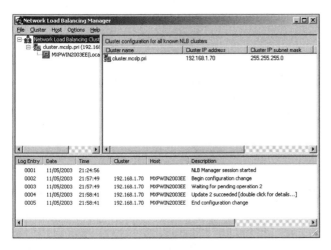

FIGURE A.1   The Network Load Balancing (NLB) Manager in action.

Two other features affect the way NLB works compared to Windows 2000, Virtual Clustering, and multiple NIC support.

Virtual Clustering

Past versions of NLB spread requests across a cluster according to the IP address and port address range on a global basis. Although technically this made administration of the cluster easier, it also limited a cluster to a very specific range of Web sites. In particular,

- Each member of the cluster was limited to supporting the set of traffic defined by the cluster.

- All members of the cluster had to support traffic for all the Web sites or applications they hosted, even if you didn't want all Web sites to be load balanced.

- You could only block all applications on a cluster member, not just specific applications.

To address these problems, Windows Server 2003 includes a new feature called Virtual Clusters. Virtual Clusters take into account the preceding problems and provide a number of solutions:

- Cluster IP addresses can be configured with different port address ranges, allowing one cluster IP address to redirect to a particular application being hosted on a specific port on each member. For example, IP address 192.168.1.20 could refer to port 80 hosted Web sites on the cluster members, whereas 192.168.1.21 refers to port 8080 sites.

- Traffic for a Web site or application can be filtered out on a cluster member basis, allowing upgrades on a single member with the cluster to take place without shutting down all other applications on that member.

- Cluster member level affinity allows you to assign different hosts within the same cluster to handle specific Web sites or applications. For example, AppOne could be hosted by members one, two, and four, whereas AppTwo is handled by members two, three, and five.

Multi-NIC Support

Within Windows 2000, it was not possible to bind the NLB service to any more than one network card (NIC). This limited clusters to handling a specific set of Web sites within a given IP address and hardware environment.

In Windows Server 2003, each NIC is attached individually to the cluster, allowing you either to connect multiple NICs to the same cluster or to configure multiple clusters using the same machines but different NICs.

Cluster Service

Cluster service provides failover capability for two or more servers within a given cluster. It cannot be used to improve the performance or response times for an application.

Typically, the nodes in a cluster are connected to the same shared storage solution, such as a RAID device, which is used not only to store user data, but also to share the *quorum*, which contains information about the cluster and how it operates. Nodes are not attached to each other except through the network and the shared storage device.

Each machine in the mode communicates a heartbeat to the other nodes, which indicates the node's availability. The moment the heartbeat of the primary node dies, the next available node in the network takes over the services the primary node was handling.

PRECONFIGURED CLUSTERS

Most OEMs will set up and provide clusters using approved hardware, preconfigured and tested to support the application you have in mind. Personally, I'd recommend this as the best solution for creating a new cluster, because getting it wrong can lead to data corruption and unstable services that might lead to a more unreliable installation.

New Features

The biggest change in the Cluster service is that both Enterprise Edition (previously Advanced Server) and Datacenter Edition support 8-node clusters. However, the Cluster service will only create clusters of nodes running the same OS edition—that is, all nodes in a cluster must be running either Enterprise or Datacenter Editions; you cannot mix and match the two.

Other new enhancements, briefly, are

- 64-bit memory support in both Enterprise and Datacenter Editions, allowing for up to 4TB of memory per node, particularly useful for SQL Server installations.

- Terminal Server support, although active sessions cannot be migrated during a failover.

- Majority Node Set (MNS) clusters enable clusters to be set up without using a shared storage device. Instead, Microsoft supplies the quorum resource. This allows for geographically dispersed clusters—for example, two database servers in different locations, cities, or even countries. You can use the same system in installations in which the ultimate storage requirement is not critical—for example, in a network-oriented system where data is ultimately transferred to or logged to another device. However, because there is no shared storage device, it's not possible to share user data across the cluster.

- The Cluster service is also now installed by default, but not activated; you don't need to separately install the Cluster service.

- Remote Administration enables all aspects of the cluster to be configured remotely. Changes to drive letters and physical disks are also replicated to active terminal server client sessions.

- The command line tool, cluster.exe, enables scripting and automation for cluster management.

- Support for a larger quorum, 4MB instead of just 64KB, allows for more file or printer shares.

- Active Directory (AD) integration. Clusters can now be registered in AD as a single computer; clusters can be identified, published, administered, and accessed by their cluster name, not their individual node names. Because a cluster is a single node, Kerberos authentication can be enabled on the cluster.

- Network status is taken into account when deciding which node to switch to in the event of failover. Previously, if a node lost network communication, it would retain control of the cluster even though other nodes in the cluster couldn't connect to it. Now, a node must have an active public network interface before gaining control of a cluster.

- Rolling upgrades allow nodes to be taken offline and upgraded while the other nodes continue to provide failover support, meaning that there is less downtime.

 WANT TO KNOW MORE ABOUT CLUSTERING?

If you're interested in learning more details about how clustering has changed in Windows Server 2003, check out *Microsoft Windows Server 2003 Delta Guide* (ISBN: 0-7897-2849-4).

IIS 6 Resource Kits Guide

The IIS 6 Resource Kit follows the tradition of Microsoft releasing additional tools and utilities for one of its applications. Typically, these are designed to augment the facilities of the original product, present solutions that would otherwise be difficult to develop, and help with security and administration.

The IIS 6 resource kit is available free from the Microsoft site (http://www.Microsoft.com/downloads). You can install the kit on Windows Server 2003 and Windows XP (useful for checking details).

The aim of this appendix is not to give you full details on all the components of kit, but to give you an overview of the major benefits and features of each component. For full details, see the guides that come with the resource kit.

Apache to IIS 6 Migration Tool

If you are migrating a Web server installation from Apache to IIS 6, this tool will help with the process. It can migrate Web site files (graphics, HTML, and so on) and configuration data (from httpd.conf and .htaccess files) to an IIS 6 Web server.

What it cannot do is migrate dynamic applications or databases from the source host to the destination. It doesn't install Perl or Python for you (actually, Perl is a requirement) and it won't handle all the directives from the Apache host.

However, it does automate the process, and for many sites it will offer a much cleaner and more effective solution for handling the migration. Because the solution is automated, it's more likely to migrate sites consistently. If your Apache host has more than a few virtual hosts, or you have a number of Apache hosts, using the migration tool will be a much more efficient method.

▶ A closer look at the specific capabilities and limitations of this tool can be found in Chapter 8, "Migrating from Apache to IIS 6" (**p. 137**).

For full details on using the tool, read the migration tool instructions that come with the resource kit.

CustomAuth Version 1

The CustomAuth tool provides an alternative method of authentication to the standard IIS solutions, such as Basic, NTLM, and internal IIS methods.

Unlike the other methods, CustomAuth provides a standard Web form that can be customized. The login credentials are exchanged over SSL and the credential information is retained on the client using a cookie. Once logged on, clients can log off manually or a timeout value can be set.

> ### USING CUSTOMAUTH
> CustomAuth, in fact, requires authentication through SSL. You can use SelfSSL, another component of the resource kit, to generate your own SSL certificates. You might also want to use the IISCertDeploy tool, also in the kit, to back up and restore certificates.

CustomAuth can be used in situations such as public kiosks, Internet cafés, and simple authentication sites for beta test distribution, demo sites, and other situations. I don't recommend its use in production environments or areas in which security is crucial—use one of the built-in authentication schemes for these installations.

You also cannot use the system with Web gardens (multiple worker processes per application pool) or mixed authentication environments because of the way in which the initial authentication and cookie credentials system work.

IIS 6 Migration Tool

Whereas the Apache to IIS 6 Migration Tool migrates Apache hosted Web sites, the IIS 6 Migration tool works with IIS 4 and IIS 5 hosted Web sites. It can even be used to migrate IIS 6 hosted Web sites between servers.

▶ The use of this tool is covered in more detail in Chapter 7, "Migrating from IIS 4/5 to IIS 6," (**p. 119**).

IISCertDeploy.vbs Version 1

SSL certificates are not the easiest objects to work with. It can be time-consuming if you have to install the same certificate over a number of machines—for example, in a clustered or NLB environment. It's also vital that you keep a copy of your IIS SSL certificates in case of system failure.

To ease the process, you can use IISCertDeploy.vbs, a small VBScript application for extracting, converting, and deploying SSL certificates.

The program uses the *Personal Information Exchange (PFX)* format for storing the certificates.

SECURING CERTIFICATES
The PFX formats allow you to set a password to secure your certificate information. I highly recommend this in case the certificate is lost or stolen—without a password, the certificate could be used elsewhere.

Exporting a Certificate

You can export the certificate from the default Web site using

```
IISCertDeploy.vbs -e exportcert.pfx -p password
```

The argument after -e specifies the name of the file to save the certificate in, and the argument after -p defines the password to be stored in the PFX file. You'll need this password if you ever want to install the certificate from the PFX file on another machine.

Installing a Certificate to a Local Web Site

To install a certificate, you must have a certificate file from a certificate authority.

At a command prompt, type the following:

```
IISCertDeploy.vbs -new cert.cer -c cert.pfx -p password -i W3SVC/2
```

Where *cert.cer* is the file supplied by the authority, *cert.pfx* is the PFX file that you want to create in the process, and *password* is the password for the PFX File. The -i option defines the site that you want to associate the certificate with.

Installing a Certificate to a Remote Web Site

The process is very similar to installing a certificate in a local site. You just need to supply additional switches and information to tell the script which server and user with administrative privileges to use. For example, to upload the same certificate as before to the server WebServer2 as the Administrator you would type:

```
IISCertDeploy.vbs -new cert.cer -c cert.pfx -p password -i W3SVC/2
[ic:ccc] -s WebServer2 –u Administrator –pwd srvpass
```

IIS Host Helper Service Version 1

If you have an intranet and are using NetBIOS or dynamic DNS for your internal naming system, you probably already use the DNS registration system to register server and client names with the service so that users can reach your servers.

Unfortunately, additional virtual Web sites that use the host header system to appear as differently named virtual servers do not register themselves through the same services.

The IIS Host Helper Service will do this for you, however, correctly registering sites by examining the IIS metabase and sending the appropriate registration to the WINS/DynDNS servers.

To install the service, at a command prompt, change to the systemroot\System32\Inetsrv directory.

Type the following:

```
isshostsvc install
```

Once installed, you can control the service either using the net command at a command prompt or through the Service Manager MMC snap-in.

Log files for the service are generated in the systemroot\LogFiles\Iishostsvc directory.

IISState Version 3

It can be very difficult to identify the location and problem when an application is performing badly. The IISState application can help by monitoring the InetInfo.exe application and all its threads, recording the time spent by each thread in the various modes (user, kernel), and recording stack information for each thread.

IISState is primarily for use with ASP and DCOM issues and, as such, requires the use of additional tools and libraries from the Microsoft Debugging Tools package (available at http://www.microsoft.com/ddk/debugging).

You should make this application available to your developers.

IISSTATE AND REMOTE MONITORING

IISState does not support remote monitoring, but you can use it within a Terminal Services session on a remote Windows XP or Windows Server 2003 host.

Log Parser Version 2.1

Post processing of log files is a time-consuming and complex task, and a number of tools have been developed over the years, including the free Analog and commercial tools, such as Seagate's Crystal Reports.

Log Parser is a free tool that can process and report on log file information. Import formats include Event Log files, IIS log files (including the new binary format), CSV and the W3C formatted documents, as well as plain text files. Export formats include HTML/XML, and you can convert your log file data into SQL tables. You can even translate log files between the different input formats, allowing you, for example, to translate IIS logs into W3C format.

Log Parser is too complex to cover adequately in this appendix, so check the details provided in the documentation that comes with the resource kit.

 WORTH THE PRICE

Log Parser is free, and it's well worth the price. However, don't expect it to replace the functionality of full-fledged log reporting tools, such as Webtrends or Crystal Reports.

MetabaseExplorer Version 1.6

I've already demonstrated how IIS 6 uses an XML-based metabase to store configuration information. The file can be edited by hand using most text editors, but if you want a more structured visual environment, you can use the MetabaseExplorer. This provides an organized, tree-based viewer system for looking at all the properties in the metabase. You can see an example here in Figure B.1.

▶ The IIS Metabase is covered in detail in Chapter 4, "Management and Monitoring," (p. 65)—including the use of MetabaseExplorer as an alternative to using a text editor and editing the raw XML.

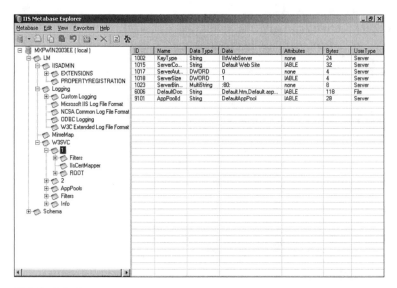

FIGURE B.1 Using MetabaseExplorer to manage the IIS configuration.

Permissions Verifier Version 1

You can verify the permissions of your IIS installation and server files using the Permissions Verifier. This makes use of an XML file to test user and group permissions. The resource kit comes with five sample templates:

- FileSystem.xml checks file system permissions.

- Registry.xml checks permissions stored in the registry.

- Metabase.xml checks permissions stored in the Metabase.

- RightsPolicies.xml checks policies.

- IIS6MinPermsVerif.xml checks server permissions.

To use, execute the PermVerif.js script from a command prompt, and use the –Config:filename argument to specify the name of an XML configuration file.

You can see an example of the output here:

```
Microsoft (R) Windows Script Host Version 5.6
Copyright (C) Microsoft Corporation 1996-2001. All rights reserved.

Using checks in file C:\Program Files\IIS Resources\
[ic:ccc]Permissions Verifier\samples\filesystem.xml
```

```
FILESYSTEM: C:\WINDOWS
FAIL: [MXPWIN2003EE\Administrator] Full:false
FAIL: [NT AUTHORITY\SYSTEM] Full:false
FAIL: [BUILTIN\Users] Read:false

All checks failed.
CheckTypes Passed: 0
CheckTypes Failed: 1
Checks Passed: 0
Checks Failed: 3
Checks Fixed : 0
```

For more details, including how to build your own XML documents, see the documentation that comes with the resource kit.

RemapUrl Version 1

RemapUrl provides remapping services to remap file and URL requests to alternative pages or servers. Once installed, configuration is through a simple text file, RemapUrl.ini. For example, to remap PageOne.html to PageTwo.html, you would use the following:

```
/PageOne.html=/PageTwo.html
```

To map a directory to another Web site, use this:

```
/Sales=http://sales.mcslp.pri
```

Installation is a three stage process—first RemapUrl should be installed as an ISAPI extension. Next, it should be installed as a wildcard scriptmap for the site on which you want to enable the remapping. Last, execute permissions should be enabled for the directory that contains remapped elements. Full details are in the documentation with the resource kit.

REMAPURL FUNCTIONALITY
RemapUrl offers slightly more functionality than the built-in redirection service, including the ability to redirect to an external site.

SelfSSL Version 1

SSL certificates are normally only available from verified authorities. This means that even if you need to test your application, you still need to pay for and install a third-party certificate.

You can get around this by using SelfSSL to create a new self-signed certificate that you can install on your server. This is useful for testing your SSL enabled site or your IIS installation if you have having trouble with a third-party certificate.

SELFSSL FOR PUBLIC WEB SITES

Don't use this tool for public Web sites because its validity and security are not as robust as those from a trusted authority, such as VeriSign. If you do use it on a public site, use it only in combination with authentication and a trusted set of users who have individually installed the certificate in their Web clients.

To install a standard certificate into the primary site on your machine, just type

`Selfssl`

To install a certificate in another site, use the /S:siteid option. To install a trusted certificate, use the /T option.

 GREAT FOR TESTING

SelfSSL is a good way to save money while testing a Web site. You won't need to purchase a "real" certificate for developer machines or for test servers.

TinyGet Version 5.2

TinyGet is a command-line based HTTP client that reports on connection status. You can use this for some basic Web site validation and testing. The output can be parsed using the Log Parser tool in the resource kit.

Check the supplied documentation for more details on using TinyGet because the number of command-line options and facilities is extensive. If you want a more rounded tool for monitoring capacity, use the Web Capacity Analysis Tool.

Web Capacity Analysis Tool Version 5.2

Testing servers to monitor their capacity and capability to handle multiple connections is a difficult task to achieve manually. Sure, you could have 100 people all pressing Return at the same time, but you couldn't adequately test the response times to be able to use that information.

The *Web Capacity Analysis Tool (WCAT)* can do this for you by submitting multiple requests to a server and timing the responses, thereby testing the server loading and availability under heavy loads. For more in-depth tests, you can run the tool on a number of machines simultaneously and increase the overall load.

Unfortunately, I don't have the space to cover the tool in detail in this appendix, so check the extensive documentation for more information.

 WHAT'S YOUR CAPACITY?

I always try to test my Web sites' capacities before placing a new site into production. Knowing how much traffic the site can handle is a great piece of administrative information that will help you plan for the site's growth.

WFetch Version 1.3

WFetch is a simple HTTP client for testing and troubleshooting HTTP servers. Unlike a Web browser, WFetch shows the request and response header, useful for debugging, as well as the raw data returned by the request.

You can see an example of the application in action in Figure B.2. To use, simply choose the verb (GET, PUT, POST, and so on), hostname, port number, and path of the document you want to test. If you need authentication, you can also specify the details.

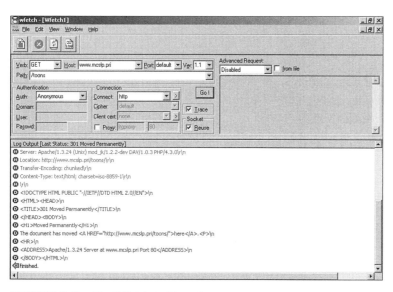

FIGURE B.2   The WFetch tool in action.

The main log output window will show the request, header response, and data as text. Again, I recommend making this available to your developers.

Index

A

How can we make this index more useful? Email us at indexes@samspublishing.com

Q - R

QoS (Quality of Service) parameters, 104

configuring application pool queue length limits parameter, 109

enabling CPU monitoring parameter, 108

enabling http keep-alives parameter, 107

limiting connections parameter, 105

setting connection timeouts parameter, 105-106

throttling bandwidth parameter, 107

utilizing http compression parameter, 106-107

rapid-fail protection, enabling, 34

recognized file extensions (security), 42-43

recovering Metabase (XML) data, 71-72

Recycle Worker Processes, 36

recycling parameters (worker processes), 35

memory recycling, 37-38

regular request period setting, 37

regular time period setting, 36

specific time period setting, 37

redirecting

directories/files in IIS, 143-145

error documents in IIS, 146

URL, htaccess files, 154-155

RemapUrl (IIS 6 Resource Kit), 181

Remote Desktop

enabling, 89

servers, connecting to

Remote Desktop Connection, 89-91

Remote Desktop Web Connection, 91-92

Remote Desktop section (Maintenance page), 86

remote monitoring, IISState (IIS 6 Resource Kit), 178

Request Queue Limit parameter, 29

request queues, 20, 29-30

requesting Web server certificates, 50-51

ResourceConfig directive, 164

responses, granular compression, 6

restarting worker processes, 115

rewriting directories/files in IIS, 144

running Web sites, IIS 5 Isolation mode, 38

S

saving Metabase (XML)

configurations, 74

copies, 72

ScriptAlias directive, 164

Secure Sockets Layer. *See* SSL

security

application pool encryption, 27

authentication, 46

Apache to IIS migration, 153-155

Constrained/Delegated authentication, 48-49

Forms based authentication (ASP.NET), 49

Passport authentication, 47-48

Passport authentication (ASP.NET), 49

Windows authentication (ASP.NET), 49

authorization, 49

certificates, migrating, 135

command-line tools, 58

directory access controls, Apache to IIS migration, 151-153

files

extensions, 42-43

verification, 46

filters, denying access, 45

FTP, 60

file sharing, 63

Isolated mode, 62

Isolated mode using Active Directory, 63

Non-isolated mode, 62

passive FTP port range mode, 63

setting isolation modes, 61

SSL, 61

hotfixes, 59

.htaccess files, migrating, 154

IIS

installation, 11, 40-41

group policies, 58

upgrades, 41

IIS 5

Compatibility mode, 54

Isolation mode, 56

IIS 6, 5

How can we make this index more useful? Email us at indexes@samspublishing.com

V - W

How can we make this index more useful? Email us at indexes@samspublishing.com

X

Y - Z